A Life Misunderstood

Developing Our Understanding of Dyslexia and ADHD: How Can We Help these Students Reach their Potential

Phillipa J Eagle

First published by Ultimate World Publishing 2025
Copyright © 2025 Phillipa Eagle

ISBN

Paperback: 978-1-923425-89-7
Ebook: 978-1-923425-90-3

Phillipa Eagle has asserted her rights under the Copyright, Designs and Patents Act 1988 to be identified as the author of this work. The information in this book is based on the author's experiences and opinions. The publisher specifically disclaims responsibility for any adverse consequences which may result from use of the information contained herein. Permission to use information has been sought by the author. Any breaches will be rectified in further editions of the book.

All rights reserved. No part of this publication may be reproduced, stored in or introduced into a retrieval system, or transmitted in any form, or by any means (electronic, mechanical, photocopying, recording or otherwise) without the prior written permission of the author. Any person who does any unauthorised act in relation to this publication may be liable to criminal prosecution and civil claims for damages. Enquiries should be made through the publisher.

Cover design: Ultimate World Publishing
Cover Artist and Illustrator: Jennifer Riley
Layout and typesetting: Ultimate World Publishing
Editor: Victoria Pickens

Ultimate World Publishing
Diamond Creek,
Victoria Australia 3089
www.writeabook.com.au

Testimonials

A thoughtful and compassionate life reflection. *A Life Misunderstood* calls for change. Change in the education of our teachers, change to the resourcing of our schools, and change to our approach to teaching and working with our kids—particularly for neurodivergent students. If we are to improve literacy and numeracy outcomes and the overall educational experience for our children, this seems a great place to start.

Karyn Corby, BA Business Psychology and Education, Managing Director Foundations for Peak Performance

I am in awe of you!

Absolutely brilliant, Phillipa! You have captured the struggles of these students perfectly, and the conflicting challenges of a school system and one-size-fits-all curriculum that, despite all the advances in diagnosis of these conditions and ever-increasing students in each classroom, does not adequately cater to them to achieve! Square peg in a round hole, indeed! I love how you have referenced the research, whilst simultaneously telling your story and your experiences of teaching these gorgeous, quirky kids! It is a fascinating read, perfectly capturing the ADHD brain as well as the struggles we often see at school and at home.

I am so very grateful that Amelie, Evan and I were fortunate enough to have found you. Your patience, kindness and care with Amelie have been more than we ever imagined, and it means so much to us all that you continue to take an interest in her sporting achievements.

Thank you xx

> Natalie Simms, Deputy Principal, Senior School, Leeming High School, Perth, and proud mother to a neurodivergent daughter

This book is a heartfelt and courageous journey through the realities of learning differences—from the classroom to the emotional core. As a mum to a child with dyslexia, I felt like Phillipa had finally put our experience into words. Reading A Life Misunderstood felt like sitting down with someone who truly gets it. The chapters on Dyslexia, ADHD, and anxiety especially resonated—they're not just informative, they're deeply human, written with honesty and lived understanding, and there were so many moments that made me stop and think, "Yes, that's exactly how it feels." I found myself nodding, tearing up, and feeling a sense of compassion for my son's experience. It's warm, raw, and full of reminders that we're not alone. I wish I'd had this book in those early days when everything felt so overwhelming.

We're lucky enough to have Phillipa on board as our son's tutor, and wow—what a difference it's made. I won't lie, the struggles

Testimonials

are still there, but his confidence is a breath of fresh air on rainy days. Little steps forward.

Whether you're a parent, teacher, or simply someone wanting to understand, this book offers insight, hope, and a powerful reminder that with the right support, our kids can thrive—and so can we.

Kylie Abbey, Financial Planner and a very proud mum to an amazing neurodivergent son

Congratulations, Phillipa. This book is so important for so many people!

It's a difficult thing as a parent to be told that your child needs to be tested for a learning disability. That conversation, that moment in time, stays imprinted in your memory, and your first reaction comes from fear. Fear that your perfect child is going to struggle for the rest of their lives, that a learning disability diagnosis may make them a target for bullies, and finally, 'how did we miss this?' The best thing a parent can do is not hesitate. Book that test, the system is so clogged and the wait for an appointment can be excruciatingly long, in our case it was nine months. A whole school year spent waiting for an appointment to be tested for a learning disability.

Once we had a diagnosis, the hard work began, and eleven years after that first difficult conversation, our daughter is about to graduate in Year 12. We don't want to think about what the outcome may have been if we had chosen to ignore that teacher's advice. Our daughter's struggle has been real, and will continue to be, but she now has the tools to overcome those daily bumps in the road and has a self confidence that amazes us, and it is all due to that first teacher, the people at Dyslexia Speld, and finally her long suffering tutor Phillipa. I say that last part with some humour as I witnessed a lot of frustration during those tutorial lessons and am forever grateful for Phillipa's endless patience.

P.S. We count ourselves among the lucky ones. Firstly, because a teacher alerted us in Year 1, secondly, because we could afford the hefty costs associated with the testing and years of tutoring.

> Peter and Andrea Ducey, parents of two daughters, one diagnosed with dyslexia and the other with ADHD.

As an educator and one of the friends referred to in this book, A Life Misunderstood provides invaluable insight into the world of neurodiverse learners. We see both the strengths and the superpowers of the student who is negotiating their learning in what feels like a 'one size fits all' learning environment. This is particularly relevant now as this is what we appear to be travelling back to in an effort to improve perceived declines in literacy and numeracy rates.

This book highlights the importance of the arts and the outdoors for the learning and well-being of not only our neurodiverse learners but all our tamariki.

I knew Phillipa as a highly intelligent, articulate young woman, and a sensitive, talented, and empathetic friend, a musician, and a natural athlete who delighted particularly in anything we could leap into. I never knew the extent of her struggles

Testimonials

to manage in an exam-based system and how I may have unwittingly contributed to those feelings.

I will recommend this book to my own family and many others who have experienced something similar on their own learning journeys.

Jennie Williams, Kaiārahi ANZAAE (NZ). Mother and grandmother to children with an SLD.

Dedication

I want to express a few words of gratitude to the people who have inspired me on this writing journey.

At the top of my list is my beloved husband Shane, himself dyslexic, who is always willing to listen, discuss, and share ideas. I dedicate this book to him, and to all the children and their parents who have trusted me to help them manage and overcome their inherent difficulties learning to read, write and spell.

Contents

Testimonials	iii
Dedication	ix
Preface – Behind the Scenes	1
Introduction – A Warning	5
Chapter One: Uniquely Human	7
Chapter Two: The Worst Days of My Life	15
Chapter Three: All in the Family	29
Chapter Four: An Emerging Teacher	37
Chapter Five: Crossing the Frontline	45
Chapter Six: Backroads & Detours	55
Chapter Seven: Ravenscroft Castle and the Damsel in Distress	63
Chapter Eight: A Sojourn in the City	73
Chapter Nine: Dyslexia Demystified	79
Chapter Ten: Time for the Spotlight	87
Chapter Eleven: Sailing Away From Sales	95
Chapter Twelve: Navigating New Directions	101
Chapter Thirteen: Embracing the Roadblock	109
Chapter Fourteen: An Idea is Born	115
Chapter Fifteen: ADHD, the child Misunderstood	127

Chapter Sixteen: The Dyslexic Disadvantage	137
Chapter Seventeen: ADHD, an Emotional Powerhouse	145
Chapter Eighteen: Connecting With Our Quirky Kids	157
Chapter Nineteen: Anxiety and the Neurodiverse	173
Chapter Twenty: The Mystery Unravelling	181
Chapter Twenty-One: Unravelled and Moving Forward	191
Afterword	201
About the Author	203
References	205
Acknowledgements	209
Speaker Bio	211

Preface - Behind the Scenes

*The simple things are also the most extraordinary
things, and only the wise can see them.*
Paulo Coelho

To be literate, the ability to read and write proficiently, is an essential skill in our modern society, which I contend to be a basic human right. A recently published review from the Australian Grattan Institute in Melbourne claims that around 33% of Australian children leave school with limited competencies in reading[1]. The blame for this unimpressive truth is laid upon the Australian education system which, the report claims, applies 'discredited theories' to the task. As I read this article, I reflect that this is not a new truth, where have they been for the last 30 years?

In 1996 the first international Adult Literacy and Life Skills Survey (ALLS), was conducted with a sample of residents

---

[1] Education - Grattan Institute , One-third of Australian children can't read properly as teaching methods cause 'preventable tragedy', Grattan Institute says - ABC News

aged fifteen to seventy-four-years throughout several OECD[2] countries. In Australia it was concluded that approximately 40% of adults present with literacy and numeracy skills that are inadequate for some ordinary everyday activities. School evidently did not do it for them either! The results were similar for both New Zealand and Australia. Ten years later, the 2006 survey recorded similar results.

For years, the debates have raged, which method is most effective for the teaching of reading? Is it whole language, structured phonics, or balanced literacy? Almost twenty years since that last ALLS survey, the current system continues to fail a significant number of our children!

I am extremely outspoken in my belief that the common approach to teaching reading, writing, and spelling has been inadequate for a long time. Many of us have become literate despite poor teaching, but too many have not. This poorly informed teaching approach has particularly disadvantaged those with learning difficulties such as Dyslexia, serving to compound their difficulties at school, and consequently impacting negatively on other areas of their life and wellbeing.

As the Grattan article suggests, individuals with significant literacy difficulties at school commonly become a problem for their teachers. Without effective help and support they are frequently disruptive as they attempt to avoid activities they struggle with. They become disenchanted with school, doubt their abilities, and develop negative self-beliefs, which may lead them to make poor choices in the future. As adults they can face huge challenges finding gainful employment and too many

---

[2] OECD: The Organisation for Economic Co-operation. Better policies for better lives | OECD

ultimately fall foul of the law. Denny, (2023) suggests that poor literacy is a strong indicator for future criminal behaviour. In a study of current prison inmates, a recent Auditor General report[3] found that a significant number of inmates presented with low or minimal literacy, with many demonstrating learning difficulties such as Dyslexia.

A quick scan of any classroom will likely reveal a significant cohort of challenged learners (10-20%), who, without appropriate support, may never achieve their intellectual potential. Lack of ability cannot be blamed for our impoverished literacy scores. Amongst those who suffer the greatest disadvantage from poor teaching methods are those with Dyslexia. These children may have extraordinary brains yet find the interpretation of graphics inordinately difficult, and as a direct consequence, battle with concentration and motivation. There are some physiological differences in the dyslexic brain that make learning to read and spell especially problematic, but this difficulty is not attributable to any lack of intelligence. For many with Dyslexia, Attention Deficit Hyperactivity Disorder (ADHD) is an additional challenge. Double jeopardy! ADHD affected brains face their own battles trying to meet expected learning milestones within our one-size-fits-all schooling system.

I have experienced firsthand, personally and as a teacher, how brain-based diversities can influence learning behaviour and outcomes; I am continually disappointed at the evident lack of knowledge and understanding amongst teachers and educational institutions at all levels. I am passionately driven to promote changes within the schooling systems that will reduce or remove the disadvantages faced by our neurodiverse students.

---

[3] Improving Prisoner Literacy and Numeracy - Office of the Auditor General

Introduction - A Warning

We are responsible for everything that happens in this world. We are warriors of light, and with the strength of our love and of our will we can change our destiny and that of many other people.
Paulo Coelho

I come from a family of quirky neurodiverse individuals, for whom no aspect of life can be considered ordinary. As I navigated career choices, relationships, and life in general, my quirkiness appeared to be a significant disadvantage. For most of my adult life I have struggled to understand why my achievements so often failed to meet expectations; this has long been a source of both frustration and curiosity. Was I lazy, or simply incapable?

Fortune was shining upon you when you picked up this book because now you too can share my story, and the journey through which I have discovered answers to a lifetime of questions! Perhaps I may even help answer some of yours. Yet, as entirely fascinating as it is to me, I do anticipate that some may not be so enchanted, and this is to be expected; all homo sapiens are not identical and if we were, the world would be a tedious and boring place. Nonetheless, if you find my story less fascinating in places, I apologise and you're welcome to skip over portions as you choose. On the other hand, if you know, teach, or live with Dyslexia, or ADHD (or both) I urge you to persist, and at least read the pertinent chapters, 13 - 19. For those with curious minds I have included, at the end of the book, a variety of references for you to investigate.

This book is an eclectic mix of personal recollections and academic musings. Readers can expect to be intermittently entertained, horrified, disappointed, sad, and perhaps even confused. Continue at your own risk.

Chapter One

Uniquely Human

> *I am a person that is very curious about what is going on in the world and there are a lot of subjects to write about, you meet a lot of interesting people. But one idea will be there, and it will show up without any logic. It is a book that has been written in my heart before it is written into sentences.*
> Paulo Coelho

We humans are perhaps the most wonderful creations on earth; I never cease to be amazed by the variations and diversity within and amongst humankind. Even within closely genetically connected families, whilst similarities are commonly evident, the physiological differences between us can be significant. I am a mere 5'3 in height with hazel eyes, whilst my blue-eyed brother is 6'2, and my brown-eyed sister is 5'7. Our brother was gifted enviably thick brown hair, while I was born with blonde and have forever bemoaned the challenges of my extremely untameable fine hair. These physical differences are equally matched by differences of disposition, which collectively frame our interpretation of the world we inhabit and our environment, and our experiences within it.

When reflecting on the proportional influences of genetics (nature) versus the environmental factors (nurture), recent research[4] attests to the dominance of our DNA blueprint in determining our personal character and dispositions. This explains how differences can occur, even when genetics and environmental circumstances are largely the same. Several studies have concluded that, whilst environmental factors may influence changes in our behaviour, such changes are generally superficial or temporary.

My adopted daughter will claim she has learned many of her habitual behaviours from me, and I will not argue that point,

---

[4] In the Nature–Nurture War, Nature Wins - Scientific American Blog Network

but it is clear to me that her special talents for music and childcare are most probably genetically embedded, especially as we see these emerging in her own daughter. Among siblings with a common familial environment, their shared DNA will create similarities, but there will be noticeable differences between them too; their shared environment does not create the sameness of personality or disposition. In a family of four children from the same biological origin each may display quite different natural dispositions. In my first brother's family, for example, each of his four children is undeniably creative/artistic. The older two are expressing their creativity through different forms of dance, while another is a singer-songwriter, and their brother is a painter and decorator. Their dispositional individuality led them to express their creativity genes in different ways.

The brain is central to all of this. Every thought, action, feeling or emotion, as well as our life functions such as breathing, is driven by and through our brain. Essentially, the design is common to all of us, but there are some specific physical variations which significantly alter an individual's perceptions and functional potential. For example, studies conducted on the brains of dyslexic individuals show reduced levels of activity in the temporal region of their brain, the area that supports visualisation and language processing. The ADHD brain too has structural and functional differences, particularly in those areas affecting the executive functioning skills of emotional self-regulation. They also characteristically struggle with time awareness, focus, and concentration, as well as an inability to manage distractions.

For most of us, one common environment of influence, beyond our family circle, is 'school'. Whilst not all schools are identical, they each tend to follow a common blueprint with a similar management structure and a common core curriculum. Even within the same school, individual experiences and interpretations will vary. This is the inevitable consequence of our human uniqueness. It is my observation that most schools lack the flexibility or willingness to cater to our infinite range of different brains, it is simpler to aim for sameness. This approach is at the heart of The Dyslexic Disadvantage.

Educational institutions may claim to offer the same opportunities to all their students, 'equity' they call it, but how can the one singularly inflexible system that is 'school' claim to cater equitably for all? I contend that it cannot! Standardised assessments and equity are incongruent. The non-standard student is forever trapped within an institution that, via its standardised measures, sets them on a pathway to mediocrity, or failure.

Two of the best-known but poorly understood non-standard brain types, Dyslexia and ADHD, are commonly described as learning *disabilities*, but from whose viewpoint? Should being different be a disability? If schools were more flexible and actively embraced different ways of seeing and doing, many of the neurodiverse students I know would have a more positive experience of school and not feel like square pegs. The environment itself may not change people, but I contend that, by appreciating diversity and offering flexibility within their system, a school can either augment or limit potential.

For several years now, I have specialised in teaching children who have been diagnosed with Dyslexia. Many years ago, when I began my teaching journey as a primary teacher, I was frustrated by my lack of knowledge about the condition.

Saddened by their low opinion of themselves and their abilities, I have long been motivated by a desire to advocate for these quirky kids who challenge their teachers' regular pedagogies. Many of the children I teach, or have taught, feel or have felt misunderstood, particularly by their teachers, but also by friends and immediate family. The Grandfather of one of my young dyslexic students continues to believe that his grandson simply needs to try harder.

This book began because I wanted to share what I have learned in a way that might enlighten teachers, whilst also guiding parents, grandparents, and significant others to greater understanding. This is still my goal, but as I began to organise the content for this book, something momentous occurred; I also began to realise that I too have lived 'a life misunderstood'! The reflections on things past, and new understandings that have evolved throughout the writing of this book, have helped me to answer some long-pondered questions, and serve as a postscript to my 2008 published master's thesis entitled 'Unravelling the Mysteries of the Great Learning Divide', (Eagle, 2008). That was the year I ultimately conquered my fears and achieved one of my life goals: completing a university degree.

I began reviewing and evaluating my personal experiences of school and learning, both as a student and later as a teacher, and suddenly realised that you, my reader, might gain much more from this book if I share some of that journey with you.

So, ultimately this story has evolved to become an autobiography of my learning journey from child to adult, how I have reached my current understandings about learning and teaching, and my beliefs regarding how we can more effectively meet the needs of some of our neurodiverse (quirky) learners, particularly with their literacy. As my story progressed, I realised that the telling was entirely therapeutic for me. Reviewing my experiences in depth triggered a 'reliving' of them, ultimately leading me to a profoundly new viewpoint. Researching, recalling, examining, and analysing the intimate thoughts and memories that inspired this book has been both healing and revealing for me; perhaps it can be for others too. In sharing my very personal educational journey I invite you to be encouraged, inspired, and informed. From wherever you sit whether you are a teacher, parent, sibling, another 'quirky' human, or perhaps all four, I hope you may draw some positive, possibly identifiable connections to your own experiences, and that these connections will lead to raised awareness and understanding that will help other 'quirky kids' and those who work with them.

This is a tale of my passage to understanding, one that has taken me more than half a lifetime. The *misunderstandings* that have preceded this epiphanous moment form the basis of the first part of my book. As I share and reflect upon my life experiences within and throughout the system that is largely responsible for preparing us for life and work, I am unravelling more mysteries of the great learning divide.

Chapter Two

The Worst Days of My Life

> You drown not by falling into a river,
> but by staying submerged in it.
> Paulo Coelho

For generations now, the intelligence or worthiness of any man or woman is commonly measured and judged by their academic achievements; more store is set on school grades, university degrees and successful career paths than any other area of human endeavour. Learning to read and write is the cornerstone of our school achievements, laying the foundations for the skill set that will form the platform from which we build and demonstrate our educational accomplishments. University qualifications continue to be the penultimate goal, and success at this level is viewed as the pinnacle of our academic achievements.

My first brother once told me that they, my siblings, looked up to me, the oldest, as the clever one, the smart one, the 'academic' of the family. The clear implication here was that they viewed themselves as less so. This surprised me, and ironically, I did not share their belief. From my perspective, I was an academic failure who always felt ashamed of my somewhat limited school achievements, which I attributed to both a lack of ability and insufficient effort. I passed only two subjects in my final secondary school examinations, English and French. Evidently, I didn't try hard enough! My apparent lack of effort and attention were regularly acknowledged through the teachers' feedback on my report cards. Examples include: 'needs to make a more sustained effort', 'more concentration required', 'capable of a better result', 'more careful attention required', 'a determined effort needed', and 'has not made sufficient effort'. My woeful examination results and, until much later, minimal tertiary qualifications have been the source of half a lifetime of shame, disappointment, and regret, for me.

Even in our early teens, many of my contemporaries appeared to have clear goals for their future, but my aspirations were vague at best. I have spent most of my working life leaping from one job to another, forever seeking that perfect match. I quickly became bored if the work was repetitive. Geographically too, I have leapt between regions and countries. I am in awe of friends and colleagues who, from the beginning, have made successful and long-term commitments to their chosen careers.

"School days are some of the best days of your life," goes the saying. I don't know who began that lie, and I'd like to put them straight! Unquestionably they were *not my* best days. My first brother also did not enjoy his school days; he once told me he felt school was, for him, like 'doing time'!

In accordance with the socially expected norms, at the age of five I was marched off to my first school. And marching I did, for two miles down the road to the local country school. Even at five, my mother encouraged some degree of independence and self-reliance; however, in case you are about to accuse my dear mother of neglect, I assure you that my walk was always accompanied by older and more responsible others.

This inquisitive, cheeky, talkative four-year-old, who my parents frequently called 'chatterbox', was looking forward to her fifth birthday and the beginning of her school adventure. My parents and grandparents had nurtured my innate love of books and learning, and I already owned a substantial library. I relished the nightly bedtime reading sessions with my father, especially

The Worst Days of My Life

enjoying those books that fed my wild imagination. At a tiny two-teacher country school of 50 or fewer children, I was initiated into the wonderful world of learning, a world with four specialist subjects, comparison, competition, assimilation, and normalisation. In this well-established production line of 'sameness' where attendance is compulsory, performance measures standardised, and delivery, even today, somewhat culturally and intellectually biased, my formal schooling began.

Memories of my earliest school days are sketchy, but certain things stand out to me. I recall being excited about my first day at school; I also recall I was so anxious and fearful in this strange environment that before the morning break I left a puddle on my chair because I was too afraid to ask to go to the toilet! The teacher must have noticed the puddle, but no one came to see if I was okay, and I embarrassingly bore the damp reminder of my unfortunate mishap for the remainder of that day.

During my first weeks of school, I learned a great deal more than reading, writing and arithmetic. I learned that, whilst it is important to do well, it is also imperative to conform, something I have never excelled at. I was never intentionally naughty, but my creative brain and impulsiveness frequently led to disapproval. I learned that I possessed some aptitude for sport, particularly running, and racquet sports, but I did not enjoy team games, especially if one had to endure the tedium of waiting for a turn.

Winners in sport became popular and often won privileges too. I learned to judge myself against others, and I learned to wear labels, which were more often derogatory than favourable. I learned that I did not fit well with the crowd and often felt more comfortable alone; other children could be unkind, and friendship was not freely offered. I found that other children can be critical, discriminatory, and cruel; being new meant being an outsider and acceptance was not automatic. To be clever academically was admirable, but it rarely led to popularity amongst peers. Appearing too clever was spurned, being 'different' in any way led to ridicule, and speaking with an English accent was *not* an advantage in my struggle for acceptance and belonging in those early days at that small New Zealand country school.

Confident and articulate, I enjoyed learning and used my excellent visual memory to advance quickly, especially with reading, so much so that I recall my year one teacher telling my mother she planned to promote me to the year two class after only six months of schooling. January is the beginning of the academic year in the southern hemisphere; being a June baby, I was already six months younger than many of my peers. This was a turning point in my school life because, although apparently capable, I was, from that point on, forever significantly younger than most of my classmates, which did little to improve my social integration.

While I was chronologically between six and nine months younger than many of my classmates, I have since realised that I was also younger emotionally; this was especially noticeable once I reached double digits. I have attributed many of my later struggles at secondary school and university to this. On reflection, I was always a bit of a square peg; the 'me' that lived inside my head existed in a different reality much of the time and I never quite felt comfortable with my neurotypical peers. I wanted to be liked, to have friends, but sometimes it became all too hard, and I would withdraw into the safety of my own imagination. Perhaps that is why, in the early years, one of my best friends was an imaginary one!

Changing schools can impact academic learning progress in the early years but even more significant is the challenge it presents to one's social skills, especially when self-confidence is low. By the age of eleven I had attended four different schools and was struggling with friendships and confidence. I wanted to fit in but more often felt like a misfit.

For ten years my parents were share-milkers, dairy farmers who contracted to manage another's farm and dairy herd and received a percentage share of the profits. These contracts were generally short-term, commonly twelve or twenty-four months. This meant I spent only a few weeks at my first school and barely one year at my second. Thankfully our next contract was longer, and I was lucky to spend four years at my third school. It was here that I formed two lifelong friendships and found some success with athletics, and other outdoor pursuits. A highlight was winning first prize at our school's agricultural day events with my dear Romney lamb, Bonnie. Her love for me was unconditional and unwavering, she followed me everywhere.

It was at this school that I discovered the depth of my mathematical ineptitudes. Our teacher's favourite daily warm-up activity for mathematics was 'mental arithmetic', a short test that required us to manipulate numbers to solve mathematical problems in our heads. We recorded our answers in the back of our arithmetic (mathematics) exercise book, but all calculations were to be solely done in our heads, no written calculations were permitted. The teacher would write ten questions on the board and give us a specified time to complete the answers, just *one minute*, I recall! When time was up, it was common practice to exchange our book with a classmate and check each other's answers. I was lucky to finish even *half* the questions. I now understand that this activity required that we use our working memory to calculate the answers. (More on working memory in Chapter 9.) My capacity for this activity was limited and the whole experience was humiliating. Given more time, less pressure, and a paper and pencil, I knew how to calculate many of the answers. However, the prescribed time limit, combined with the need to calculate and hold numbers and calculations in my head, sent my brain into a frantic spin and my working memory into overload! That 'mental arithmetic' gave me a huge headache and nearly drove *me* 'mental'! For those who successfully answered all the questions there was praise and respect from our teacher. I was just ten years old, and I was resigned to the fact that I lacked the aptitude for such games and gradually gave up trying. Avoidance was my strategy; if I didn't attempt the activities I couldn't fail.

Sustained concentration, such as that required for mathematics, did not come naturally and my head was often out the window with the birds, but I was creative and loved writing stories and poems. I think I impressed my teacher with my three-stanza poem about the nearby cheese factory we visited, so much so that he submitted it to our local paper. I cannot recall it all now, but I remember it began like this:

Sixty-four pounds in leaps and bounds
Gets sorted and packed,
And sent on its rounds.

I displayed a strong disposition for music and dance from an early age, and I was thrilled when my mother offered me the opportunity to try both piano lessons and ballet classes. The ballet came to a halt when we moved to my fourth school, but I continued with my piano lessons. My first piano teacher, Mrs. Clark, possessed the demeanour of a no-nonsense major general, which I found terrifying, and it dampened my initial enthusiasm for the piano. I was relieved when we found Mrs. Logan. She let me find my own level and allowed me to choose pieces of music that I enjoyed. I grew to love the piano, but that old fear of failure meant I did not dare to attempt any exams. I learned to play well enough and played many of my pieces from memory. I could read the musical notations, but I had extreme difficulty following the notations fluently as I played; I would continually lose my place. It often felt like the notes were jumping about across the page. I could have faked it for my set pieces, but 'sight reading' was a compulsory part of the exams and I felt defeated before I began. Later I added the guitar and singing to my repertoire, but just as a hobby, no exams, my chronic fear of failure ruled that out.

My departure from school number three had marked a plateauing in my educational motivation and performance as I adapted to a new environment, expectations, and friendships. I held no clear vision of my future and the only subjects that truly caught my interest were music, art, and drama. This next move came when I was five months into Form 1 (Year 7). It was another two-teacher country school; the headmaster and his family lived in the schoolhouse on the grounds. Many of my new classmates were children of long-established families, some with parents who had also once attended the school; many friendships were long-standing. Once again, I was an outsider. Additionally, puberty was rearing its ugly head with its usual emotional inconsistencies. Despite these challenges, I was generally happy to attend school, especially when swimming or athletics were on the schedule, but the young girl who once impressed her teachers with her quick and agile mind was beginning to slide away into 'averageness' academically.

After eighteen months at my fourth country primary school, it was time to take the gigantic leap into an urban secondary school. From this point onwards the quality of my school life deteriorated markedly.

Of all the changes in my life thus far, secondary school was the greatest shock to my system. Suddenly, I was navigating my way through multitudes of new faces and large, unfamiliar buildings with endless corridors of dingy, uninspiring classrooms; this was indescribably overwhelming. Until this point, my school experience had been limited to small country schools with three teachers at most. This secondary school, situated in the heart of suburbia, was populated by hundreds of students, and we had different teachers and classrooms for every subject. One of my overriding memories is of the mental and physical exhaustion I experienced at the end of those long days. Just getting to school was a veritable endurance test that began at 6.30am with a mostly downhill bicycle ride to the end of the road to catch the bus, followed by a forty-five-minute bus journey.

By morning-teatime, I was struggling to maintain focus and sometimes slipped out to the toilet just to rest my brain! School days seemed endless, so much to absorb and remember, I soon began to wonder at the point of it all. Most afternoons I was so exhausted that I was barely conscious of the bus ride home. Sometimes I fell asleep! To make it worse, at the end of that afternoon bus ride was a torturous, mostly uphill, bicycle ride to get back to the farm; some afternoons that journey seemed insurmountable. This should have been a welcome change of scene, but the whole day had been such an effort, I had nothing left in my tank.

Today my bicycle could be in a museum. There were no gears on my sturdy steed; it was a solid and hefty frame that could likely survive being run over by a bus! Ride it or push it, that old bicycle took a lot of effort to move!

For me, our farm was paradise, and nothing was ever better than spending a day at home. I loved everything it offered, whether it was haymaking, hacking out to the back of the farm to pull ragwort, a virulent, noxious weed, or even getting up at 4.30am to help Dad fetch the cows in for milking. Almost anything would have been more inspiring, but school was an unavoidable fact of life that, through necessity, I did my utmost to manage. Out in the country as we were, even to play 'hooky' was difficult, the only available transport was shank's pony, and there were spies everywhere! I recall one such occasion. A friend who frequently cycled the same route had encouraged me to dawdle on our way down to the bus thus engineering that we arrived just in time to see it disappearing into the distance. It was a beautiful day, so we decided to walk. Realistically, this could have taken all day, which I would have enjoyed far more than school, but disappointingly, we were intercepted by a kind neighbour on her way to town who offered us a ride, which of course, we simply could not refuse! Incidentally this neighbour was not only familiar with both our families but also an inveterate gossip. By the time I returned home that afternoon my story was prime news, and my mother was not impressed! The subsequent disciplinary consequences were inevitable. No! You shall not go to the ball!

As much as I hated it, school was an inescapable reality, so I tried to focus on the positive aspects. I found much enjoyment and some success with music, art, athletics, and swimming, and I discovered an aptitude for writing and singing. Undoubtedly, my greatest secondary school memories are of my time in the choir. We were fortunate to have a talented and inspiring music teacher and choir master who produced some exceptional orchestral, choral, and operatic performances. Our very professionally produced production of 'Joseph and His Technicoloured Dream-Coat' received public accolades, and we even travelled to perform in Australia. After his passing this music teacher had a new theatre in the town named in his honour. The benefits, socially, emotionally, and educationally from participating in these extraordinary events were immeasurable. Music provided me with vital inspiration and motivation, still does. I was especially fond of singing to the accompaniment of my guitar. This quiet and unassuming student once gained temporary fame when she performed her own unique rendition of *The House of the Rising Sun* to her entire school at morning assembly. This proved to be a huge shock for my teachers and peers; I recall it was a particular source of amusement to my geography teacher at the time. For a while, my nickname was Janis!

Despite these pleasant interludes, my days at secondary school remained, without doubt, some of my worst!

I satisfied my stubborn streak by wearing my uniform very short and refusing to wear the standard-issue hat, which resembled an upside-down bucket! I still hate hats. For the most part, however, after the Janis interlude, this quiet and unassuming student kept out of the limelight. I focused on being a conscientious student and, generally, kept up with my work expectations; however, aside from English, my results were increasingly average, with only modest bursts of brilliance. I was continually striving to do better, but it was a constant and mostly unrewarding struggle. My school reports, whilst never bad, contained many comments indicating that teachers believe my achievements did not accurately reflect my potential and that I could improve my status by working harder. I had serious doubts about this. I continually tried, but despite my genuine attempts to make sense of the copious notes and references presented to me by the various subject teachers, I was frequently so overwhelmed by the requirements that I didn't know where to begin. Most of it seemed irrelevant to me then, and there was far too much to remember. My characteristic inattentiveness and distractibility made it a constant challenge to focus on anything that didn't inspire or entertain my interest. Keeping up with weekly work schedules was stressful enough, but the end-of-year examinations were a living nightmare. Doing well in secondary school was always my goal but, ultimately, successful is *not* how I would describe my secondary school years.

A Life Misunderstood

Chapter Three

All in the Family

> When we love we always strive to become better than we are, when we strive to become better than we are, everything around us becomes better too.
> Paulo Coelho

Our family did not regularly attend church, but our upbringing was firmly embedded in the fundamental Christian principles. My father especially held strong views on right and wrong. Respect for parents and elders was high on the list as was honesty and integrity. We all understood that stealing, envy, or selfishness was wrong and learned that showing kindness to others, even in the face of adversity, was the better thing to do. One of my father's favourite mantras, do unto others as you would have done unto you' (Matthew 7:12), has been a constant voice in my head, especially at times when I felt I was being treated badly or unfairly. Being naturally quiet, sensitive, and somewhat shy, bullying, teasing, and other unkind acts of judgement and discrimination were not unfamiliar to me, especially in my junior school days. I wanted to be liked, to have friends, to have fun, but I was not always good at choosing the right friends. I recall one day of misery when three girls I thought were my friends pushed me down onto the ground and held me there while taunting me verbally. How dare I think I was good enough to be their friend? I didn't fight back; I could never intentionally be unkind to others, no matter what they had done.

My parents' attitudes and expectations influenced my behaviour and outlook in both positive and negative ways. Any indications of laziness or 'stupidity' were scorned by my father. The use of common sense was applauded, as was the ability to engage in polite conversation with others, whether family, friends, or guests. My natural aptitude was to be cheerful, but I was a highly sensitive and empathetic child who readily picked up on others' feelings, and especially if they were negative, assumed they were caused by me. I had no idea how to deal with the overwhelming guilt that would consume me, so would withdraw for a time. My mind was always busy, and I tended to act impulsively, which often got me into trouble. The resulting admonishment would send me down into a dark hole of shame and regret; I would hide away in my room until something jolted me out of my cloud of misery.

Both parents valued education and wanted us to do well. My father held high expectations for us, especially regarding linguistic correctness and broad general knowledge. His own education had been interrupted by World War II, but he remained a lifelong student with an expansive field of knowledge and interests. We were encouraged to read widely, pay attention to local affairs, and question anything and everything to learn. I constantly aspired to be good enough to receive his praise but rarely did. Being naturally inquisitive, I asked many questions of him, but often his responses left me feeling deflated or even stupid; don't you know that?', or 'don't they teach you that at school?' were common responses. He applauded inquisitiveness but encouraged wider fields of research, particularly books; I have followed his lead in this and now possess quite an extensive library.

Our mother was more encouraging, although her own memories of school were not entirely positive. She admitted to being better known for making mischief than for her academic achievements, and, like me, had enjoyed drama, music, and art. Her confessions to mathematical mediocracy served to support my developing view that I was similarly genetically wired and had little hope in that subject! From an early age I appeared to have a natural aptitude for writing; creative writing especially offered an escape from the increasing sense of failure I felt. Mathematics was another thing altogether. When my third form (year 9) mathematics teacher could not adequately unravel the mysteries of Algebra to me I slowly faded into the background. "It's a pity that Phillipa, a quiet and pleasant student, is not a mathematician", he wrote in my report card. Well, who needs algebra anyhow? With the meanings and identities of x and y remaining unsolved, I entered my fourth form year (year 10) programmed for ultimate failure in mathematics.

To relieve the tedium, I, encouraged and supported by two equally disheartened friends, instigated 'the absolute failure challenge'. The goal was to achieve the lowest possible score in any test, whilst honestly attempting every question. Our teacher, freshly graduated from university, simply accepted our self-proven ineptitude, and largely ignored us for the remainder of the year. We gained the impression that he held greater interest in analysing the recent rugby results with the boys anyhow. Given that mathematics is generally considered one of the two key foundational competencies I am appalled no attempts were made to remedy this dastardly situation and I was allowed to complete my schooling without further mathematics learning. At the time I was relieved, but later, when faced with the dreaded 'statistics' paper at university, which, surprisingly I passed, I realised how, if presented differently, and in a meaningful context, I could easily have grasped the necessary fundamentals.

Fifth form (year 11) was an important year, being 'school certificate', later to become the National Certificate of Education (NCEA) Level One. 'School Certificate' was attained by completing a series of nationally accredited end-of-year examinations, the passing of which then qualified one to enter sixth form (year 12). School days were interminable and draining for me. Some days I struggled to concentrate on anything and by the end of each school day, I was mentally and emotionally washed up. One of my greatest challenges was managing the ever-increasing quantities of homework. I would far rather be out helping on the farm than studying for a science test! Procrastination was my most faithful companion; I struggled to find the motivation to begin, then I struggled to get organised, then I struggled to stay focused. When I didn't know where to begin, I distracted myself with more enjoyable things like playing my guitar. The examinations terrified me. Faced with high expectations and limited timeframes, a swirling panic would consume my brain, hindering all logical thought and causing me to doubt even that knowledge I once was certain of. English was the only subject I performed well in, although my aptitude there did not create immunity from extreme examination stress. I recall one instance when, ironically, I became severely distressed because I could not remember how to spell the word, *anxious!*

On reflection I think I suffered a kind of depression for much of my fifth and sixth form years. Six subjects, endless random notes, diagrams, information, and data to be crammed into my distressed and overwhelmed memory for the sole purpose of regurgitating them in some meaningful order for a test or examination. Battling perpetual fatigue and lack of connection with the material, I constantly fought the desire to give up. It didn't help that I struggled to get to sleep each night which meant I was constantly fighting tiredness too. Sleep deprivation does the brain no favours.

I closeted myself away in our homeroom, or the library most lunchtimes, doing what I loved, writing. I produced short stories and poetry and engaged in fascinating conversations with our form teacher of the time. She was a major ray of sunshine in an otherwise exhausting and seemingly futile routine. There is no doubt in my mind that teachers can play a critical role in their students' educational journeys. I was fortunate to have had two exceptional teachers whilst at secondary school. Both taught English, one was also the Deputy Principal. The characteristic that made each of them special to me was their ability to truly show an interest in each of us as individuals, and to take time to listen. One made me, and all her students, feel comfortable by sharing some aspects of her own life. This not only created context for learning but allowed us to know her as an authentic human being, rather than solely a font of knowledge and assessor of academic 'worthiness'. The other fostered my particular interest and talents in reading and language, lending me books from her personal collection. It was this teacher who was most influential in my decision to apply for the teacher training programme at University.

I was strongly drawn to the arts and fantasised about becoming an actress or writer, but those ideas were shelved in the face of two hurdles, a lack of real opportunity at that time and my mother's abject disapproval. Knowing she had been an avid thespian in her younger days I found this attitude surprising and disappointing. Mother emphatically expressed her belief that acting was a hobby, not a 'real' career option, so the dream was abandoned, and I became a teacher. One interview led to three years of full-time study, followed by a year in full-time practicum, and ultimately, my Graduate Diploma in Primary Teaching. That I completed those four years was nothing short of a miracle, or perhaps it can be attributed to a stubborn determination not to give up! Trusting the integrity of my school reports, I believed I simply needed to work harder.

Chapter Four

An Emerging Teacher

> *Everything tells me that I am about to make a wrong decision, but making mistakes is just part of life. What does the world want of me? Does it want me to take no risks, to go back to where I came from because I didn't have the courage to say "yes" to life?*
> *Paulo Coelho*

It was a very young and naïve sixteen-and-a-half-year-old who left school to begin her teacher training diploma. I was surprised to be accepted at such a young age, especially given my mediocre academic success thus far. Acceptance came from one in-depth interview and references from my school. I must have impressed them with my verbal acuity, because my academic results would not have thrilled them! With university being a couple of hours away from home, I was obliged to pack up a few belongings and move into the university student lodgings, The Halls of Residence. Ignore the fanciful name, this place was more like a jail than a comfortable residential hostel. For a young country girl used to a habitat filled with pasture, trees, and animals, this was an enormous step into a dark cold abyss. Our lodgings consisted of a minuscule bedroom shared between two, furnished only by two single beds and a shared wardrobe. "Barely large enough to swing a cat," my father remarked when he saw it. We were each allocated a small study desk in a room next door, which was shared with three others; for one so easily distracted, this was not an ideal set-up.

Meals were provided at the hostel cafeteria in another building, and most of the food they produced bore little or no resemblance to anything I had ever eaten or wanted to! Soggy, tasteless, over-cooked vegetables, rich meats drowned in putrid gravies, and rubbery white bread that I would hesitate to feed to my pigs, all proved less than appealing to me and I rarely dined in the student cafeteria. I regularly drew upon my emergency rations, apples, cheese, mixed nuts, and some of my favourite dark chocolate to keep me going.

My overwhelming memories of this place are of cold, dampness, and all-consuming loneliness. I was a fish out of water; an eagle trapped in a cage; I couldn't wait for Friday afternoon and my escape back to the farm. Each week I became increasingly reluctant to return to that bleak residence, but with a lot of willpower and an enormous dose of motherly encouragement, I did. As she regularly reminded me, an incomplete qualification was worth nothing, so I soldiered on.

At the end of my first year, I gratefully escaped those dingy Halls of Residence. For the remainder of my three-year sojourn, I was house sharing with other students, not always in total harmony but indisputably superior to those dark halls.

Whilst I enjoyed much of the academic work, especially English and Music, I continually struggled to maintain sustained periods of concentration. No matter how hard I tried, it was a constant battle to remain focused on the important task at hand. My mind was constantly busy and could, on a whim of its own, wander off to a totally unrelated place. Meeting assignment deadlines was a serious challenge. Consulting with my diary and its reminders of multiple projects and due dates, I often succumbed to a frozen state of overwhelm, struggling to know how and where to begin. My brain was full of ideas, but under the pressure of high expectations within limited timeframes, I had difficulty organising my thoughts into a logical and coherent written presentation. There were no computers then, no spell-check, no cut-and-paste options and all assignments were hand-written. I frequently burned the midnight oil and wasted a forest-load of paper on re-writes!

Curiously, when I discovered a topic that truly interested me, I could focus on it indefinitely. One of my most fascinating and engaging projects was an English assignment requiring a critical review of a book of our choice. By chance, I discovered a most engaging book titled "Dibs in Search of Self" (Axline, 1964), which I read with urgency; I could not put it down. It tells the true story of a boy who had been emotionally abandoned by his parents. A part of me has always been drawn to the stories of children who face extraordinary odds.

Dibs (not his real name) lived at home with his parents, but as the tale reveals, they were so busy with their professional careers that they had no time for him; this sad little boy spent most days alone in his bedroom while they were busy at work. The parents substituted love for expensive toys, of which he had many. Dibs didn't speak and remained non-verbal throughout his pre-school years, so his parents believed he was mentally handicapped.

The first and most impressionable years of Dib's life were spent predominantly in isolation so when he started school this deeply troubled child was unable to participate as he should. Dibs was non-verbal. He did not know how to communicate with others or develop friendships; he hid under the teacher's table until he was collected at the end of the day. This boy's story moved me to tears. I received an A for that assignment and almost got it in on time, just a weekend extension! Dib's story did have a happy ending by the way, but it took almost ten years and the support of an exceptional psychologist.

Applying and maintaining concentration was always my greatest challenge; I needed a strategy. I discovered that listening to classical music helped me focus, and it still does. I began to 'closet' myself away in the music section of the library, where I was able to don a set of headphones and block out most other distractions whilst I worked. This strategy slightly improved my scholastic output but did no favours for my social life; unlike so many of my fellow students, I simply could not balance the two.

Our written assignments contributed only half our marks; there were also the dreaded end-of-year examinations. For me these were torture. As I read through the papers, I was overtaken by a sense of panic whereby whatever my brain 'knew' seemed to evaporate into thin air. The harder I tried the greater my distress. Each page became a blur as words would dance across the page; in my panicky state I would often forget familiar spellings, which only served to intensify my anxiety levels. Although I frequently felt like giving up, failure was not an option I was prepared to accept. However, everything seemed to take me so much longer than it did everyone else, and I was always tired. I envied my friends who passed all the exams with very little apparent distress. As difficult as it was, I persevered and endured; giving up would mean certain failure and the associated shame, which would do nothing for my already fragile self-esteem.

I recall my father was never one to make or accept excuses. If something was difficult or challenging, one just had to step up a bit. In the face of pain, be it physical, emotional or mental, one must give that pain but a few moments of your time and energy before moving on with the present and all it demands. I witnessed his personal commitment to this philosophy on several occasions, most notably on the loss of his beloved cat 'Boy', then later, on the death of my dear mother, his wife and life partner of almost fifty-five years. With my father's mantra playing in my head and a stubborn determination not to fail, I persevered.

Thanks to a very patient and understanding head of school, and a couple of re-sits, I eventually completed my assessments, and attained my Diploma in Primary Teaching, but I was not proud of my results. I had passed, but not with the 'Honours' grade that many of my friends attained and I did not feel confident to commit to the extra papers which could have transformed my diploma into a degree. My difficulties organising and focusing impacted on my confidence and inhibited the realisation of my full academic potential.

Chapter Five

Crossing the Frontline

When we first begin fighting for our dreams, we have no experience and make many mistakes. The secret of life, though, is to fall seven times and get up eight times.
Paulo Coelho.

Before being awarded our diploma it was a requirement that we serve a 'probationary' year in a classroom, an experience I looked forward to with a degree of unease. Our practicum sessions thus far had been no more than three weeks in duration, and I suddenly felt inadequately prepared. I'm naturally anxious in new situations, especially where I know my actions will be observed and counted, and I have an unsettling habit of playing things out in my mind overnight, rather than sleeping. I began my practical year full of eager determination, and plenty of creative ideas for engaging my eager young students, but in practice, the reality was a million miles from how I had imagined it would be, and my level of anxiety was off the scale. For a class of ebullient seven-year-olds, remaining still and orderly in their seats was not natural but it was the only classroom system I understood. Whilst I did not have to deal with anything extreme that year, there was always unexpected behaviour and the physical and vocal exuberance to manage, whilst still staying on task, and delivering the required curriculum content.

Behaviour management was never my forte, nor did my teacher training provide any helpful clues. I recall discussing 'behaviour modification' and positive reinforcement strategies, but how exactly does one begin to modify behaviour in a large group of children? Is it even a realistic option? Interruptions, disruptions, and distractions to the planned programme were frequent and sent my head into a spin. It was my understanding that the best teachers always had their class under control, and any miscreance was swiftly dealt with. Evidently there was a lot more to this teaching thing than I yet knew. I was eternally tired—physically, emotionally, and mentally exhausted come the days end, and completely crashed at the end of each term!

Somehow, I survived my first year in the classroom and even enjoyed much of it, but each Friday I left school mentally and emotionally consumed. Temporary distractions like the annual visit from the traveling drama group, police road safety team, inter-school sports day, or practising for the end-of-year Christmas Show were welcomed. Some of my most unforgettable moments include a headlice outbreak at the school, learning how easily they spread and their preference for clean hair, staying calm and focused during every new teacher's nightmare - the school inspector's visit, and catching hepatitis B from one of my young students, which put me out of commission for about six weeks.

Working with children can be extremely rewarding but managing a full classroom of twenty-six of them is an extraordinary phenomenon, particularly for an inexperienced teacher. As a provisional teacher, I was especially conscientious with my formal planning and record-keeping. Originality and creativity were my hallmarks. I was continually generating opportunities for learning and exploration delicately blended with moments of fun. Children being children, and me being me, the recorded outcomes of my attempts read more like a comedy of errors. My meticulously prepared sessions almost never went as planned. The planning process was time-intensive, especially with my perfectionist tendencies, and often kept me up late into the night, but the implementation of my plans was quite another thing; creative adjustments mid-session were a regular happening.

Nothing we learned in our three years of theoretical training had adequately prepared me for the multi-faceted classroom management aspect of teaching! Neither did I have any knowledge or understanding of children's learning differences or difficulties, or how to accommodate them within a classroom, and I had virtually no understanding of any potential relationship between the two. What should I do with fidgety Anthony who cannot sit in his chair for more than a few minutes at a time, or curious Louise whose mind frequently wandered and needed my constant attention and guidance to stay on task? What led the apparently clever Matthew to distract everyone with silly antics whenever a writing task was required? Where is Max, and why has he run off again? Why is Jenny still struggling to read the simplest text in her third year of school, and how can I help her? How can I help Stephen, the constantly overactive child who spends more time under his chair than on it, stay focused long enough to learn?

I had not heard of Dyslexia, Dyspraxia, Autism (ASD) or Attention Deficit Hyperactivity Disorder (ADHD). I realise now that the more puzzling behaviours I witnessed were probably manifestations of some of these conditions, but no one was discussing such things at the time.

With my probationary year completed, I was now a fully qualified primary teacher, ready to spread my wings! This very country girl had no desire to live or work in an urban environment. My three years closeted in a city university had been torturous, so I had successfully applied to complete my probationary year in a country school not far from my family home. The best thing about this was that I got to spend every weekend at home on the farm.

The following year, my first year out as a fully qualified classroom teacher, I was lucky to be appointed to a unique type of country school known as a 'District High School'. This was one of the few such schools in New Zealand at the time, its point of difference being that it provided education for students from the beginning of primary through to the end of secondary. The school sat within a farming district, in an area characterised by its harsh, somewhat rocky, undulating landscape, and was populated predominantly by sheep and cattle farmers. Their work requires physical fitness and stamina, practical knowledge and skills; for the farmer, success is supported by astute planning and organisation. Politically and practically, farmers tend to be conservative, hard-working, and driven. They expect the same from their children.

It was at this school that I first recognised the unforgiving nature of our education system; I began to acknowledge the limitations of a classroom teaching situation which does not create equity for all, and where intellectual ability is not a guarantee of academic success. Amongst the twenty-nine mostly eager young faces that graced my classroom was a boy for whom each school day was an exhausting feat of endurance. Ben presented with chronic concentration and attention difficulties, was socially withdrawn, and struggled with all reading and written activities. Bearing some resemblance to the Dibs I had read about at university, this boy would frequently hide under desks or behind shelves to become invisible to avoid participating in class activities. Ben was quiet and introverted. His avoidance strategies, while not usually overtly disruptive, included uncooperative and anti-social behaviour, silent defiance, or furtively disappearing from the classroom. Yet this boy did not appear unintelligent. Was he lazy? I felt a strong connection with him and wanted to help. I honestly did not know how to deal with this; nothing in my teacher's training provided any clues, but I tried. I adjusted my expectations and broke his activities up into smaller chunks, discussed each task with him first to be sure he understood, and allowed him a free-choice activity break at the end of each abbreviated activity. It wasn't perfect, but as he began to trust me, his attitude did begin to change, as did his output, which was a huge relief to me.

The system required every teacher to undertake regular, formal assessments of children's reading, writing, and comprehension skills; their results were calibrated and recorded against their formal progress reports. These assessments not only determined a graded score but also led to each child being allocated a 'place' in his or her class. At the end of each school term, these rankings, accompanied by a more subjective teacher assessment of 'effort', were included in individual reports provided to parents. This troubled boy's mother was so focused on the fact that Ben was still placed 29/29 that she was unwilling, or unable, to celebrate his recorded improvements. I have often recalled my experience with this child and realised that he may have suffered a specific learning difficulty such as Dyslexia, ADHD, or both. Tragically, neither I nor his parents had any clue, so he did not get the help he most needed. I was only his teacher for one year and was unable to follow his school journey any further; I hope he ultimately found the help he needed.

Despite a greater awareness of such "outside the box" learners, many of today's classroom teachers will admit they feel poorly prepared to help their struggling students; their understanding about the mechanics of learning, especially early literacy, remains vague and incomplete. Notwithstanding the evidence for phonics, the Reading Wars continue across the globe and the 'whole language' movement, which I believe has led to our poor literacy levels, continues in many schools. The 'whole language' approach is underpinned by a strategy known as 3-cuing. It requires emerging readers to guess unknown words from pictures and context clues, and, through repetition, begin to memorise the words, which is very demanding on the working memory.

For our ADHD and Dyslexic students, the whole language approach generally fails them when their working memory slips into overload and they are unable to keep up. They are only too aware they are failing but trying harder doesn't help. All too quickly that slippage becomes too great and, believing themselves less able than their peers, they give up. Without specialist intervention, these children will never catch up, falling further behind each year. For the lucky ones their parents will spend the extra money and time on private tutelage to help their child rebuild their shattered confidence and develop the reading and writing skills they need. Unfortunately, until schools and teachers are fully equipped there is no alternative and the younger these children are identified and supported the better, and faster, they can turn around.

It is my observation that, despite apparent greater awareness, few schools are even marginally equipped to address the specific learning needs of those with differently wired brains, those clinically described as neurodiverse. The problem is exacerbated for many of these children who are exceptionally skilled mentally and linguistically, yet measured by their written work, they are treated as 'special needs' and denied the mental and academic stimulation they need and are capable of. These students are present in every school. 'Attention-Deficit-Hyperactivity-Disorder' (ADHD), Autism-Spectrum-Disorder'

(ASD), and Dyslexia are possibly the most well-known, but Auditory Processing Disorder, Developmental Language Delay, Visual Processing Disorder, Dysgraphia, Dyspraxia, and Dyscalculia also feature in today's classrooms. For a child with any of these conditions, school is always more effortful than for their neurotypical peers, then, because their regular school cannot meet their learning needs, we ask them to attend extra schooling! Our education system is far from equitable for these children.

Pondering my educational journey, from student to teacher, to adult student, has led me to conclude that it is the educational systems and processes, more particularly the rigid commitment to uniform inflexibility, conformity and compliance that has failed so many, including me, and left us feeling like hexagonal pegs in very neatly rounded holes, so many damaged egos, so much unrealised potential.

Ultimately, as I continually unravelled and reinterpreted these personal experiences my disenchantment with our school system became absolute. There is nothing just or fair about their offerings. Essentially the staunch and unbending principles that underpinned the education system our parents and grandparents experienced have continued to dominate the modern-day approach to education. Despite the gallant efforts of some, academic scores continue to be valued above technical or even artistic achievements. Whilst strong literacy skills are a foundational requirement for every subject, the predominant methods employed to teach reading and writing have not proved effective, and most remedial programmes have simply offered more of the same. An example of this is the Reading Recovery programme. Despite an apparently increased awareness of learning difficulties such as Dyslexia or ADHD, it grieves me to observe that so many of our neurodiverse students are just as disadvantaged today as they were in my parents' schooldays.

Chapter Six

Backroads & Detours

> *Tell your heart that the fear of suffering is worse than the suffering itself. And no heart has ever suffered when it goes in search of its dream.*
> Paulo Coelho

My interest and passion for teaching was never in doubt, I loved working with children and still do; however, classroom teaching has so far proved to be a very bad match for me. I found that primary teaching required a level of mental and emotional energy that I struggled to maintain; by the end of each day my brain felt like a wrung-out sponge! There were always the 'out of the box' children who took up lots of my time but whose needs I felt I had not adequately served. Sleep deprivation was a constant, unwanted friend. The serious illness I developed towards the latter end of my second year of full-time teaching is likely testament to the level of anxiety and sleep deprivation I battled.

At the end of that exhausting year, I travelled to England for the six-week summer break to stay with my paternal cousins in Broadstairs, where I enjoyed a traditional English Christmas, although the snow arrived a little late. I also had some fun with other relatives, some of whom I had never met. Of course, it was winter in Europe at that time, and in February I returned to a beautiful New Zealand summer with such pasty white skin that friends asked if I'd been unwell.

I arrived home refreshed but not excited to return to teaching for a third year. When the ministry offered me a position, I reluctantly agreed. This posting was at a smaller traditional primary school on the outskirts of a country town, not far from my previous post. I was given a delightful class of 7 and 8-year-old children, my favourite age group. The staff were welcoming and supportive but still I found the job mentally and emotionally overwhelming and constantly battled exhaustion. How did other teachers manage to make it look so effortless? Perhaps they had brains that were not so easily distracted, better able to stay on topic and did not get or become so overwhelmed by the demands of multi-tasking and the asynchronous noises of the classroom and surrounds. By the end of each school day my loosely wired brain usually felt like a racing car with a burned-out engine, flat tyres, and dysfunctional brakes. Essentially, I enjoyed the job and hoped it would become easier. The skills and ideas were abundant, but I constantly struggled to sustain the necessary mental focus and energy. In the end my favourite part of the day was my bicycle ride home, wind in my hair (no helmets then), followed by a mind-soothing stroll along the beach, or a swim.

At the conclusion of that contract, I reviewed my future options. Having no idea what I should do next, I packed up and abandoned my rented beach house and flew back to England to spend some more time with my erstwhile distant family and muse upon the possibilities. Ultimately, I stayed there for five years!

As I dug my feet deeper into the beautiful English countryside, I realised that if I was to stay on a while, I needed an income. In the attractive and historic town of Glastonbury in County Somerset, I found a part-time job in a craft shop where I learned how to make colourful and sweet-smelling candles and produce decorative plant-pot holders, wall-hangings and fly screens with macramé. Enjoyable and calming as it was, the income was a pittance, and I needed to afford rent and food, and put fuel in my car.

I had intended to move away from classroom teaching, but when the need for work re-surfaced, teaching became the most accessible option. Supply teachers (relievers) were in demand, especially in secondary schools, and New Zealand-trained teachers were well respected in England, so I tried it for a while. Well, it was a bit like getting back on a horse that was still bucking! I quickly discovered that nothing had changed; for me, teaching was still a mentally and emotionally exhausting profession. I thought middle-secondary might be more straightforward, but what I discovered was the opposite. The older the kids, the greater the challenges and the more mental and emotional energy required. However, stubbornness is a personal trait with which I have been blessed, and the income was very attractive. Rather than give up, I decided that, just as my teachers had written in my school reports, I simply needed to try harder!

I was living with my mother's sister and her family in the tranquil village of Middlezoy, in County Somerset. My first relieving appointment was at Haygrove School in nearby Bridgwater. It was a very new school when I was there, having only been established for about five years. I became a regular there, covering English, History, and Religious Studies for years 9 and 10, and Level One French for year 9. I don't recall any of the kids being especially terrible, but they frequently delighted in pushing me to the limit with their creative behaviours. For a relieving teacher, I believe this is a common experience.

I recall a particular occasion when I was facilitating a year 10 history class. The topic was 'The Holocaust', and the scheduled activity was to watch the documentary. From the beginning the whole class was noticeably unsettled and slow to focus on the film and the thought-provoking questions I had posed for them to consider whilst watching. The narrative is far from benign and is one historical saga that, along with the Rwanda story, always brings me to tears. For these cheerful students, I'm certain the stories and experiences the film exposed were a million miles from anything any of them could imagine and getting the attention of the young twenty-something relief teacher was a far more entertaining prospect. While the boys were stirring up cheeky trouble, the girls were urging them on. From some clandestine corner of the room, several small and tightly folded pieces of paper were being dexterously catapulted by means of a rubber band! I was at my wits end trying to restore calm until finally my resilience dissolved, and I walked out! However, that is not the end of the tale.

One smart individual fetched the headmistress and after a briefing from her (which I did not hear) I returned to a quiet and delightfully cooperative classroom. This diminutive woman obviously had their respect and was astute in her interpretation of the situation. Experience, and intuition, count for a lot, especially when it is supported by the polite regard that an effective principal generally commands, and a relationship of mutual respect. Interestingly, those boys were forever courteous, respectful, and friendly towards me for the remainder of my time at that school.

The minimum school leaving age in England at that time was 16. One of my regular classes at Haygrove was a group of 15-year-olds who had pretty much given up on their educational journey. They were simply biding their time until they turned 16 and could sign out of the system that failed to inspire them. I felt some despair for these kids, most likely beset with learning difficulties that had never been identified or addressed. These kids had tuned out of school and had little interest in the curriculum, so I turned the session into a discussion and debating group.

I persevered a little longer, and even enjoyed much of my time there, until, in a moment of total insanity, I accepted a permanent position in a special boarding school that catered exclusively for children with Dyslexia and other learning difficulties, my special area of fascination.

Chapter Seven

Ravenscroft Castle and the Damsel in Distress

We must struggle for our dreams, but when certain paths prove impossible, it would be best to save our energies in order to travel other roads.
Paulo Coelho

Ravenscroft School was situated near Farleigh Hungerford, a small and enchanting village close to the Frome River in Southwest England, not far from the beautiful city of Bath. I say *'was'* because I have since learned that this school closed in 1996. Apparently, most staff and students were then transferred to Farleigh College, where the special education work continued.

When I first encountered Farleigh Hungerford it featured a pub, a few cottages, and farms, but not much else. The pub served as a perfect place for my colleagues and me to escape the rigours of school life and debrief. Like many an English country inn, The Hungerford Arms was comfortable and homely, more like a large living room than a public house, and, in winter, the open fire provided a welcome respite from the brisk night air. It took us approximately half an hour to walk from the school, a time to share the problems of the day and solutions for tomorrow. After a pint or two of Scrumpy any problems were resolved, or forgotten, and the walk back took no time at all!

Ravenscroft, a somewhat unconventional school, operated from a large and stylish country house known locally as Farleigh House and sometimes Farleigh Castle. It was owned by the school headmaster and his wife. They lived in one of the cottages on site, along with their two enormous Irish Wolfhounds that followed them everywhere. I especially recall how those hounds entertained and distracted us during the tedium of morning assemblies. At times it was a veritable biology lesson!

Originally a preparatory school, Ravenscroft had established a specialist teaching unit catering for children with Dyslexia. Over time, the demand for places in this unit had increased so significantly that when I joined the staff, the school had been re-classified as a special school for children with Dyslexia and other learning difficulties. Enrolments included students up to school leaving age. All students were boarders, and most staff lived on site too.

I was employed to teach English and general studies to children aged between seven and ten. Manageable, I thought, and fun, I considered. After my struggles with behaviour in regular schools, I relished the idea of a small class of eight to ten students, believing it would be a piece of cake! In that regard I was seriously delusional and, ultimately, I came to realise that accepting this appointment could rate as one of my most irrational decisions ever!

I believe I was genetically predisposed to become involved with Dyslexia. At this time, I was not yet aware that my youngest brother had been diagnosed but the little I had heard about it fascinated me. During my brief employment at my father's old school, King's Bruton, I was interested to learn that one of the students in my senior house group was dyslexic. I was aware that reading and writing was difficult for him, but I had little understanding of the mechanics of it. For his final exams, this student was allocated a reader-writer and extra time to give him a more equitable chance of success.

What is 'Dyslexia'? That was a question I had no clear answers to. I knew only that it was characterised by difficulties with reading and writing but, whilst I was strongly motivated to help these children, I had no specific strategy at my fingertips! Another issue that required understanding was 'Attention-Deficit-Hyperactivity-Disorder' (ADD, or ADHD), a condition that existed alongside Dyslexia in several of the Ravenscroft students. Of this malady my understanding was even more limited; I knew only of extreme behaviours and difficulties sitting still, and like many then and now, believed ADHD was a problem principally found in boys. ADHD in girls was and still is frequently overlooked because their most common behaviours (easily distracted and inattentive) are frequently interpreted as intentional laziness or simply choosing not to pay attention.

So here I was, fuelled by optimism but floating on the edge of ignorance. I won the position because I was a qualified primary school teacher and therefore considered well-equipped to help students improve their reading and writing skills. As I was to learn, the dyslexic brain does not view written words through the same lens as a non-dyslexic or neurotypical, and it can take them longer to process the information. In those Ravenscroft days, with limited knowledge and understanding about the specifics of Dyslexia, my strategy was to simply do, perhaps a little more intensely, what I would do with any students of a similar age and stage, it was all I knew. Our resources were limited, and by today's standards, primitive. Each classroom featured a large blackboard and chalk—yes, really! If we were lucky, we could borrow an 'overhead projector' (OHP), and occasionally we could access a Video Tape player (VHS). Copies of any paper-based material were produced using that dinosaur of technology, the Gestetner. For the benefit of younger readers, the Gestetner Cyclograph (full name) was an early duplicator that made copies using a stencil and ink. I had a love-hate relationship with that machine! Paper jams were commonplace, especially when the job was urgent, and my fingers were almost permanently stained with purple!

Some of the best work happened when I discovered that my young students were fascinated by dinosaurs; decades later, as evidenced by my grandchildren, their popularity has never diminished. In a flash of brilliance, I decided to plan some learning activities around this and combine natural history with English writing, spelling, and reading skills, and of course some art. I had not yet heard the term 'integrated learning', but on reflection, that is precisely the method I employed. The flying dinosaur, Archeopteryx, was a favourite with my class. Our classroom was soon decorated with colourful drawings, posters, and dioramas, with the occasional bit of writing, and numerous three-dimensional cleverly created prehistoric creatures floating above us.

I soon realised that, even when fully engaged with a topic, concentration time for these children was limited, and there was no predicting when the wheels were going to come off, which they did, frequently. This was mentally and emotionally exhausting for me, but not surprising once I better understood the learning and developmental challenges these students constantly faced. Experience has taught me that change and uncertainty can exacerbate their eccentric behaviours whilst establishing routines can help to reduce their anxieties.

I am by nature reserved and patient; my brain works best in an environment that is organised and orderly, which is what I endeavoured to create and maintain in my classroom. My endeavour was but a dream, the reality was more like alphabet soup. Moments of order and harmony were few and far between with these colourful kids! Extremes of noise and disorder can trigger a state of total overwhelm within the quirky brain, and I also struggled in such moments. With these kids it was a continual battle to manage the wheel-less moments appropriately.

One memorable day I am ashamed to say my increasingly tenuous resilience dissolved completely. Robert, one of my 11-year-old boys, was on Ritalin for his ADHD, as were several other students at that time. The Ritalin effect comes with a time limit (no slow release then) and once it wears off you get to see the raw power unleashed. One afternoon Robert came in after the lunch break in an overly excitable mood and was unable to sit still or even try to focus on our class activity. He had likely missed his lunchtime dose. Encouraged by a classmate, he proceeded to undertake gymnastic activities with his chair and used his desk as a climbing frame, which had the rest of the class in stitches. Robert remained unresponsive to any of my attempts to refocus him. At the precise moment my quickly dissolving patience snapped I had the chalk duster in my hand and, as I swung around to admonish him (again), the duster flew from my hand and unbelievably hit him square on the forehead! I'm sure a judge and jury would not believe me, but it was totally unintentional; if the offender hadn't been standing on his chair at the time, it may well have simply hit the wall!

The whole class was immediately very quiet, and I, horrified at my impulsive act, quietly regained my composure, checked that the boy was okay, and carried on. Young Robert was stunned into silence, but I was relieved to note there was no evidence of serious injury. For several weeks I waited with bated breath for the call to the headmaster's office, or the parents' letter of complaint, but neither eventuated, thank goodness.

The high energy factor was a regular feature with these kids, and they could not be expected to sit still for long. A teacher needed not only to be well-prepared but also to have one or two alternatives ready in case things threatened to turn to custard. Over time these overly rumbunctious kids were sapping my energy and spirit faster than I was able to replenish it; one morning my coping mechanisms dissolved completely. A couple of kids welcomed me with the usual polite "good morning, Miss" as I walked into the foyer, but I could barely find the energy to respond with even a weak smile. By the time I had climbed the stairs to the staffroom, I felt like a flattened amoeba. I collapsed into the nearest empty chair and inexplicably dissolved into tears; like a puppet with her strings cut, I was broken, and I simply could not pull myself back together.

I felt shocked and somewhat ashamed about that, and the chalkboard incident still played on my mind, but in truth, I was seriously burned out! After a hot cocoa and a debriefing with my colleagues, it was decided I needed a stress break. Working with a group of children is always demanding, even more so when they each have quite specific and different learning (and emotional) needs and the propensity to episodes of radical behaviour. My mental and emotional capacity to endure was falling seriously short. My head told me it was straightforward, I just needed to try harder, get more organised, try new approaches, and get more sleep! I now recognise that it takes an ever calm, wise and confident teacher to stay grounded amongst continual chaos and unpredictability, particularly when one is dealing with something they have a minimal understanding of. I admired the seemingly unflappable approach of one of my colleagues, whom the children adored, and wished I could be more like him. I never saw him appear ruffled and he handled their emotional eruptions with the gentleness of a saint. When dealing with an overly exuberant child he would give a welcoming smile while gently saying "bless you my child".

It was clear that I had become mentally and emotionally burned out; far from being grounded, I was drowning! My 'stress-break' included lots of sleep, listening to my favourite music, and many walks in the surrounding hills, after which I did feel renewed. It was not a quick fix. I shocked myself one day when crossing the street from my flat; I thought to myself, 'If a car is coming, I don't care if it knocks me down!' My doctor was extremely understanding, he asked a few questions, listened to my ramblings, and offered some little red pills which in the end I did not take. Even in my depressed emotional state, the possibility of becoming reliant upon drugs to cope was not appealing. The music and nature walks soothed my soul, and the long sleeps recovered my energies. I returned to work three weeks later, determined to stay on top of things, and for the most part, I did.

I still found the job exhausting, teaching these children was fun too, but very intense. After my burnout interlude, some of my thoughtful colleagues kept a considerate eye on me. Somehow, I completed the year without further incident, but, despite my best attempts, even after a year in amongst it, I still felt decidedly underqualified regarding the Dyslexia and ADHD; I did not have a proven or effective strategy to help these children.

Leaving Ravenscroft, I found myself feeling unsettled. I think I had, figuratively speaking, reached a crossroads. My connections with England had deepened during my time there and, as well as enjoying time with my extended family, I had made many good friends. I had grown to love everything England offered, the quaint villages with their ancient cottages and hidden histories, the lush green pastures, and heather-pink rolling hills, the character filled public houses (pubs), and the endless opportunities to freely explore coast to coast via some of the well-trodden paths that make up England's sometimes spectacular National Trust Walks. They say home is where the heart lies, and mine was becoming fragmented. My parent's long-ago decision to make New Zealand their home meant I and my siblings had grown up without knowing our cousins or our true homeland, a gap I had now filled, but the connection to parents and siblings was pulling me back toward the Land of the Long White Cloud. There were just a few more things I needed to do.

Chapter Eight

A Sojourn in the City

> On your journey to your dream, be ready to face
> oasis and deserts. In both cases, don't stop.
> Paulo Coelho

A reconnection with another cousin led me to London. I am not a natural city girl and found this vast metropolis both fascinating and terrifying. For me, this city's saving grace was the regular and normally efficient public transport system, especially the underground trains known as the Tube. My terror subsided once I realised how easily one could navigate in, around and beyond this expansive city, and I decided to prolong my stay.

With my passion for the arts and London's plentiful entertainment, my sojourn in this city ultimately proved therapeutic; I was not quite ready to leave. Through my cousin, Alison, I found temporary work at the newly opened Barbican Arts Centre where I was privileged to experience some of the world's best music, art, dance, and theatre as one of the perks of the job. The Royal Shakespeare Company set up their home base at the Barbican, and the concert hall was filled every night with patrons bathing in some of the greatest classical music and musicians of the time. Initially I worked as a security guard—yes, really! Each shift I could be observed strolling my designated area of care, torch in one hand and hand-held radio in the other, monitoring a selection of the multiple entrances to the Barbican Centre. Those who knew me struggled not to laugh at the idea of a diminutive 5'3, (48kg) 24-year-old female fending off any criminally intentioned intruders. Fortunately, there were no incidents of that nature, although, in truth, I would have welcomed some excitement as the job was intensely boring. However, it proved a fortuitous step towards a more interesting job in the administrative hub of the barbican when, one afternoon, I was asked to help in the Booking Office, and this led to a regular casual position.

I loved working there, so I hardly noticed that I was frequently working ten or more hours a day. My job was mainly clerical, selling theatre and concert tickets on site, as well as managing telephone bookings; the work itself was not what held my fascination so much as the refreshingly eclectic mix of people I met. Many were art or music students, theatre assistants, or actors between roles. Whatever their talents, most of them I would describe as creative, out-of-the-box, quirky individuals; there was always entertainment inside the office as well as out. I felt right at home there. When seats were available and our office manager was in a generous mood, we were privileged to attend some performances free of charge. Some of my best musical memories during my year there include an evening with the Danish musical comedian, Victor Borge, and hearing Rachmaninov's Piano Concerto no.2 played by renowned Russian born pianist, Vladimir Ashkenazy.

One day my beloved Barbican job came to a sudden end. The Barbican Administration Centre was now fully established, and our manager and her deputy were streamlining operations. They no longer needed so many casuals, and as one of the last in, my priority status was set. Oh well, I was preparing to return to New Zealand, wasn't I?

At that time, North Bridge House Preparatory school, on the edge of Regent's Park, was advertising for a relief teacher for one term, so I remounted that old horse. In total contrast to Ravenscroft, North Bridge House focused primarily on building academic excellence and core values of self-discipline, teamwork, leadership, and creative thinking. I am certain there was some Dyslexia and ADHD here too, but as every child in my class was considered academically exceptional, they obviously were not failing. I recall no significant behaviour issues, even when we took the children across to Regent's Park playground for a supervised break. It was a dream job, and if they'd had a permanent vacancy, I may have been tempted, but it was my time to leave.

I purchased my ticket home to New Zealand and still had enough for a sun-filled holiday in Greece, and its stunning islands, followed by a trip to Malaga and Cadiz in southern Spain, to visit my Uncle John and Aunt Catherine who had recently bought a casa there and retired to be artists in paradise.

Next stop New Zealand: I was missing my family, particularly my young brothers and sister who were growing up so rapidly I felt I hardly knew them.

Chapter Nine

Dyslexia Demystified

> *When we're interested in something, everything around us appears to refer to it (the mystics call these phenomena "signs," the sceptics "coincidence," and psychologists "concentrated focus," although I've yet to find out what term historians should use).*
> Paulo Coelho

I cannot recall exactly how or when my fascination with Dyslexia began but this special interest of mine has followed me throughout my life, a strangely synchronous connection that has popped up in different places and moments. When I returned to New Zealand, I discovered that one of my brothers had been diagnosed with Dyslexia! My youngest brother displayed exceptional talents in technical drawing, but his written work was painfully slow and filled with misspellings and grammatical inconsistencies. His difficulties have persisted into adulthood.

Evidently, Dyslexia is a genetically shared brain difference frequently found in more than one family member. A French scientist, Stanislas Dehaene, in his 2009 book, discusses the 'cerebral origins' of Dyslexia; he also deliberates on its genetic heritability. I began to consider these possibilities within my own family. If one of your children has Dyslexia, there is a strong possibility that it can be traced to a parent or grandparent; I recommend keeping an eye on their siblings, too. Each of my siblings and I struggled with many aspects of schooling, but our youngest brother was the only one who was provided an explanation for that struggle.

It was at that time I encountered SPELD. SPELD is an acronym for *'solutions for people experiencing learning difficulties'*, which might be Dyslexia, Dysgraphia, Dyscalculia, ADHD, or any other issue that may lead an individual to struggle with their school learning. I lapped up this opportunity to gather some explicit knowledge about Dyslexia and ADHD.

During a series of fascinating tutorials, we explored the human brain and learned about the extraordinary connections (neurons) that develop and grow in our brains to facilitate new learning pathways. I learned that a brain with Dyslexia is neurologically wired slightly differently from the non-dyslexic brain. A revelation indeed! I learned that some of these connections, particularly those used to recognise and interpret the symbols of language, travel a less direct route in the dyslexic brain; hence, they take longer to achieve the same reading or written outcome. Imagine walking to school every day, and rather than taking the fastest and most direct route, you must always take the longer route. You leave at the same time as your neighbouring schoolmates but will always arrive later because you have further to walk. For our dyslexic students, this usually means needing more time to read the class text, interpret the math problem, or write up the story or report. We should not be surprised when our dyslexic students are exhausted at the end of their school day.

I also learned that ADHD and Dyslexia are common co-morbidities (approximately 40%), with a diversity of presentations and several common challenges. After my Ravenscroft experience this knowledge was not a surprise. One notable commonality shared between Dyslexia and ADHD is a reduced working memory capacity. 'The Working Memory' is the crucial area of our brain that enables us to hold, process, recall and manipulate several pieces of information simultaneously to apply it to a specific task. To understand the mechanism of working memory, visualise a workspace that is constantly being cleared. This workspace is used to hold ideas only briefly whilst using those ideas to complete another task. The ADHD brain easily becomes overwhelmed as the number of items to be manipulated increases (Barclay 2016, Brown 2018). The dyslexic brain is most challenged when processing information that involves reading and writing but may also experience some difficulty with mathematics. I think back to my struggles with mental arithmetic and have a brief 'aha moment'. For the ADHD brain, where inattentiveness and distractibility constantly compromise the ability to focus, an information overload is a real and ever-present threat. Occasionally, the pressure of this overload may produce an explosive response, or at other times, a total withdrawal or shutdown. Another 'aha' moment! The dyslexic brain is characterised by inconsistency; the dyslexic student may speak knowledgeably and eloquently about a topic yet struggle to organise and express those ideas logically and sequentially. They may be able to articulate their knowledge and thoughts clearly but struggle to organise their thoughts in writing. They are acutely aware of their difficulties but often prefer not to be singled out for special assistance, preferring to persevere with some modest 'accommodations' such as extra time.

Dyslexia, like ADHD, is not a choice; it is not a temporary condition that can be 'cured'. It is a lifelong challenge. Almost all dyslexic individuals can learn to read and write, but many will require intensive, specialised, and explicit teaching to enable them to become functionally literate. As the dyslexic brain needs extra time to develop the vital neural connections required to build fluency and automaticity in reading and writing, it is no surprise that, without effective intervention, these children frequently get left behind in the school system.

Many individuals with Dyslexia also struggle with the additional challenge of ADHD. This can exacerbate their learning challenges as it interferes with their attention and focus. Some may find medication helpful; it may substantially reduce their ADHD symptoms and enable them to focus more clearly within the classroom environment. This is a temporary benefit that comes with side effects, is not a cure, and will not help with their Dyslexia. I am wary of giving children drugs and recommend you obtain more than one professional opinion before embarking on that journey. Medications do come in various types and strengths, and you may need to try more than one. Some children are uncomfortable with the changes they experience with medication. I am not qualified to debate or advise on the use of ADHD medications, but I do believe it is important for your child to feel okay with taking it, that it actually helps them without diminishing their naturally ebullient spirit.

For those who, like me, would rather not use drugs, there are strategies that parents, teachers, and the ADHD child can learn and practise. Identify the primary areas of difficulty, then accommodate and reduce the stress of time constraints by allowing extra time for preparation and completion. Adjust assessment activities and timeframes so the child feels more confident in completing the task. Review and revise the way instructions are communicated and teach them how to make effective use of calendars, diaries, and timers. Provide them with a quiet working space to reduce distractions and the opportunity for planned breaks between intense activities. While mindful activities such as yoga and Tai Chi can have a positive effect on concentration and focus, so too can a couple of laps of the field, or ten minutes on the trampoline.

Having completed my short course on Dyslexia, I decided to forge ahead with a plan. With my newly acquired knowledge and understanding about Dyslexia, I decided to follow a dream and launch my own tutoring service, providing one-to-one sessions to individuals in my own home. My students were referred to me through SPELD. Every child who came to me had received a diagnosis of a 'specific learning difficulty' (Dyslexia, ADHD, or both) from a trained assessor, and I set up a learning programme for them. I noticed that, even with similar diagnoses, each child presented differently, and my delivery needed to be adjusted accordingly.

Experience revealed that some children struggled more with auditory confusions, such as hearing the difference between the sounds of 'f' and 'th', while others had strong auditory discriminations but were persistently confused by similar graphic images, like 'p', 'q', 'b', and 'd'. I also discovered a fascinating and frustrating phenomenon whereby a student may appear confident with a skill one week and have forgotten it the next. A teacher's nightmare! My teaching sessions were, of necessity, highly individualised and facilitated plenty of repetition. Understanding that we are building new neural connections, one must allow the dyslexic brain more time to learn and practise each skill, along with lots of repetition until that skill is embedded in their orthographic memory. For progress to be sustained, they needed regular daily practice, which requires parents to become actively involved, but I soon realised that for that practice to be effective, the parents needed training too.

My students typically came to me directly after school, by which time they were usually mentally spent. No surprise, really, once you understand how much harder a dyslexic or ADHD student must work to complete the same amount, even nearly, and still achieve less than their potential. These were the days when 'whole language learning' reigned supreme and the student with Dyslexia or ADHD was not the only one to struggle, but they generally fell further than their non-dyslexic peers.

Getting started was somewhat trial and error as my needs assessment was based on the types of reading and spelling assessments done in school, an institution, and system, which had indisputably failed these children so far. I found one of the most helpful methods of reviewing a child's spelling and writing difficulties was to look through their school workbooks. In all honesty, I was flying by the seat of my bell-bottom trousers. These children had been struggling with their reading and writing since reception; I knew one forty-five-minute session per week was not going to be enough. Additionally, whilst I now understood more about Dyslexia, I was still far from being an expert, and I was becoming aware that despite being a qualified primary teacher, I had a lot more to learn about teaching literacy to struggling students. 'Whole language' principles were not working, neither was 'blended learning', a wildly concocted and far from systematic combination of 'whole language' and phonics, adopted by those who recognised some of the limitations of 'whole language' and a few of the benefits of phonics. None of this helped, I needed a better programme.

Meanwhile, it soon became evident that this private tutoring work was not only hugely time consuming, but very poorly remunerated. A handful of students was not going to pay the mortgage and put the bread on the table; I needed to put my dream on hold and find a more lucrative income.

Chapter Ten

Time for the Spotlight

> The two worst strategic mistakes to make are acting prematurely and letting an opportunity slip.
> Paulo Coelho

Office work was completely foreign to me. I had never used a computer, nor even a typewriter. Invoices and statements were something I received from the telephone or electricity company, I had never generated a purchase order, and what on earth was a 'back order'?

I was initially fascinated by my new job as a clerical assistant with a lighting manufacturing company called 'Freelite'. There was so much to learn, and I thrived on the camaraderie of my new colleagues in this small family business. Upstairs was the home of the leadership team, where unique designs were imagined and created, and crucial business decisions made. Downstairs, where I worked, was principally the storehouse for all the various components, as well as the prepared client orders ready for shipment. I shared an office with the warehouse manager where I sat on a fancy swivelling office chair learning to create job sheets, product orders and invoices. Fascinating stuff indeed! Most of the metal and brass components used to make the finished product were manufactured in Freelite's offshore factory in Samoa, and local outworkers were contracted to construct the end products, generally at home. One of my more tedious jobs was to ratify the incoming deliveries against the attached packing slips. Another tedious job was assembling brass table lamps, but this proved a convenient way to supplement my mediocre office clerk's income; each Friday I gathered a box of parts and completed the assembly at home during the weekend.

After a few months, I had the measure of the job, knew my way around the computer, and had developed good working relationships with colleagues and regular clients. Once I knew my job well, I realised much of the work was tedious and repetitive, and I began to get restless. My overactive brain was being underused and needed to be challenged.

An advertisement randomly spotted in the local newspaper sparked my interest; the Tauranga Repertory Society was seeking men and women for roles in their next production, a farce called 'Noises Off' by Michael Frayn. Finally, the chance to walk the boards, to realise another yet unfulfilled dream.

Over the next three years my amateur thespian career took off! I became an active member of both the Repertory Society and the Operatic Society, which featured my fondly remembered school music teacher and operatic society director, the famous Bob Addison. Theatrical work motivated and inspired me. I was active in at least two shows per year, which filled many hours learning lines, and songs, several evenings per week of rehearsal, then two weeks of performances for a paying audience. My uninspiring day job left my brain free to learn scripts and develop my characters.

Some of my most memorable roles included Badjelly the Witch (a Christmas pantomime), Frenchie in an Operatic Society production of Grease, and the 'clerk of the court' in Carolyn Burn's play, 'Objection Overruled'. Many of the plays were comedies, but sometimes some spontaneous unwritten comedy occurred, such as when lines were forgotten or entrances missed. The theatre became uncomfortably hot in summer, so the backstage doors were usually left open. One memorable evening, during our production of Alan Ayckbourn's play, Joking

Time for the Spotlight

Apart, a local cat wandered in mid-scene and casually walked through the set, engaging affectionately with the legs of one or two of the characters on her way across the stage. This caused some considerable mirth amongst the cast, and a wave of stifled giggles was heard from the backstage crew.

The plot of this play leaned more toward farce than comedy. My stage character, Louise, is married to the vicar who she learns has for some time been lusting after one of his parishioners, Anthea. In her misery and anguish Louise has turned to drugs and alcohol, and in this scene, she has completely lost her mind over it all. At the very moment Kitty takes centre stage, broken hearted Louise is loudly expressing her loathing of Anthea to her long-suffering neighbour, Olive. It wasn't an appropriate moment for me (Louise) to show amusement, so, at the site of the cat, I stifled my giggle by disguising it as a slightly manic wail. I later heard that the audience thought the cat entrance was intentionally staged!

My theatrical jaunts more than met the needs of my overactive brain and fulfilled my teenage dreams but it was only a hobby and came without remuneration. Unfortunately, I had to retain my day job, which, by now, I was finding exceedingly monotonous and uninspiring. I was eager to find something new.

Scanning the 'Situations Vacant' section in the newspaper, I spotted an opportunity I could not ignore. The local radio station was seeking an energetic and enterprising individual to join their advertising sales team. The job description did not sound complex, visit local businesses to secure new and maintain regular advertising contracts. I was confident the job was within my capabilities, but with no previous experience in this field, I knew I needed to come up with some unique way to sell myself.

My clever scheme involved collecting evidence from a range of local businesses about their preferred radio station and presenting the tabled results at my interview. That evening, I received the call, my scheme was a winner, and the job was mine!

The following week, I became part of the radio advertising sales team, a diverse mix of ages, genders, and personalities. One of the older and long-standing team members was also a part-time on-air personality, specialising in sport, which apparently required that many of his sales meetings take place on the golf course! Another was a young and not-long-out-of-school, outgoing and clever blonde with attitude and a name to match. Sharlene's natural gift of charm, which she used freely, ensured she exceeded her targets every month. Another was an experienced, confident, and self-assured sales professional with a refreshing British sense of humour that kept us entertained when the pressure was on. Shortly after I took up my role, we were joined by an ebullient, smart dresser who shared my name. This smartly dressed addition to our growing team, with her endless energy and enthusiasm, had already tasted success in sales elsewhere and very soon became one of our top-performing members.

I loved working at the radio station where, amongst the many interesting characters, I made some good friends. However, I soon discovered that I was not a natural salesperson. I had no difficulty establishing positive relationships with my regular clients, and I quickly picked up the key knowledge for the job. However, I lacked the consistency, the strong outgoing personality and forceful persuasiveness that generated success for others in the role. I can certainly be persuasive about things I know well and firmly believe in, but I am not comfortable asking for money or going in 'cold', and inwardly I feared rejection.

We were paid a comfortable monthly retainer, with a bonus paid for sales achieved over and above. Keeping our regular clients happy was a major part of the job, and I managed that well, but to earn a bonus one needed to increase sales beyond the regular. For this one needed to secure a significant contract, perhaps a special promotion, or bring in a new customer. The most successful in our team were on the telephone or meeting face-to-face with clients or prospects at least four days each week and regularly took home a significant monthly bonus.

My problem was one of consistency. Some days I was firing on all cylinders, while on other days I simply did not have the mental or emotional energy to be even slightly dynamic. No matter how determined I was to be different, my mental and emotional energies would see-saw from one extreme to another, and I just had to learn to maximise my 'up' moments. We were taught that selling is more about problem solving rather than persuading, however, I realised that a certain level of emotional energy is essential to establish and maintain confidence in your product or service as you seek to close the deal of the moment; some days, I just couldn't find it in myself. I was especially uncomfortable 'cold calling', dropping in on a client or prospective client without an appointment, but this was an essential part of establishing and maintaining new business.

Chapter Eleven

Sailing Away From Sales

> The adrenaline and stress of an adventure are better than a thousand peaceful days.
> Paulo Coelho

Despite my relatively mediocre performance as an advertising sales agent, I was generally happy in the job, but ultimately, it transpired that I wasn't so committed to my sales career. I had certainly found my true love in the Repertory Theatre, however, a proposal for a new adventure led me to reconsider; an offer to join an offshore sailing trip to Fiji and the Pacific Islands led me to literally jump ship.

The voyage began in Tauranga Harbour one sunny May morning. The captain and crew had prepared for a three to six-month trip, so there was some careful planning and provisioning involved. Since we were leaving New Zealand shores, the boat, a 32-foot sailing sloop, had to meet the safety requirements for Category One, and we needed to be approved for departure and checked out by a passport control officer.

One calm autumn afternoon, with regulatory requirements met, we sailed out into the blue. That first evening was close to magical. Until then my sailing experience had been limited to short trips in and around the Tauranga Harbour; this was my first experience out in the middle of the ocean with nothing to see but the sea; it was stunning. Up on deck, taking my turn on watch, I imagined being the only person on earth (or sea).

The auto pilot steered us safely through the calm seas enabling us to leave the wheel to eat and even sleep a little. Any initial anxieties I felt were being gently rocked away.

Twenty-four hours later there was a noticeable change in the atmosphere; I was about to have a rude awakening as to the fickle nature of the high seas. We watched as the clouds rolled in and listened as the weather channel warned of an impending storm. How worried should we be? I recall wishing we could head back to land but well understood that is never a wise move once a storm is up; a careful sailor knows it is safer to stay far from shore in rough seas.

Seemingly out of nowhere, a few threatening clouds turned the previously calm seas into a veritable tsunami; soon, rather than sailing we were surfing! As the boat was tossed about by the strengthening wind and waves the captain ventured forward to lower and fix the mainsail, then into the hold to retrieve the drogue, a funnel shaped device towed behind the boat to slow it down and help to maintain some stability.

Was I afraid? Just a little. As I, in my full storm kit, sat huddled close to the cabin, I realised there was not a lot one can do in such circumstances. We were entirely in God's hands. The few times I dared to glance behind me I wished I hadn't. Powerful walls of foaming water pursued us like a hostile army. These colossal foaming waves, propelled with terrifying force, more than doubled in size as they approached, threatening to swallow us completely. I took a few deep breaths, averted my focus to the chart, settled in under the Bimini (the cockpit cover) and prayed for it all to go away. With the mainsail down and headsail trimmed tight we rode the storm for the night and hoped for the best.

As dawn broke and squawking seagulls swooped overhead, I tentatively ventured out into the cockpit. The seas were tamed, we breathed a sigh of relief - we had made it, and apparently totally unscathed.

What followed was a complete contrast to the twenty-four hours nightmare we had endured. The hostile winds evaporated, leaving us in a state of absolute calm. For a sailing vessel this is not ideal. Luckily, we had motor power for such an eventuality.

Or did we? As it transpired, the starter motor was *not* starting, and we were becalmed and drifting. We had a serious problem; we could not risk continuing our journey without a starter motor. The skipper worked his magic, and we gained motor power again, but the unreliability of the starting mechanism meant a postponement of our trip. Our nearest landfall was Auckland, New Zealand.

Chapter Twelve

Navigating New Directions

> *If you think adventure is dangerous,*
> *try routine; it is lethal.*
> *Paulo Coelho*

The fate of the starter motor was uncertain, a rewind or a replacement. Both came at a cost so while the decision was in the air, I went off to look for work but continued to live in the yacht moored at the marina. While I grappled with the possibilities, which weren't abundant, I decided to undertake a night class in television drama, I hadn't quite let go of my thespian dreams. This led to a couple of one-off contracts as a TV extra. It paid quite good money; I spent a couple of hours on set as part of a crowd scene and received $100 for my time. I thought this could be a good wicket and was excited for the prospect, but sadly, the contracts were few and far between. Apparently, I was in the wrong age bracket! The truth was that I was the right age, but I was blessed to look younger, so I shouldn't be too disappointed. Sadly, that was where it ended, another dream shattered.

With the starter motor problem still unresolved, and winter approaching, the sailing dream was also quashed. A coincidental meeting with an old radio colleague from my previous job ultimately led me to a less creative but more reliable job, another radio station but in a mixed role of clerical administration and publicity rather than sales. This was not my ideal job either, but I still didn't know what was. By now my employment history was reading like a disjointed chronicle of short stories in which the main character chased rainbows but repeatedly failed to find the pot of gold.

One day, down at the Auckland waterfront I befriended a woman who was waving her husband off on a six-month fishing voyage, leaving her and her twin girls alone. From that day we became firm friends and regular café companions. One day she drew my attention to an advertisement for a teacher on a life skills course for unemployed adults. 'It sounds easy', she said. 'Just teach them some job interview skills and help them prepare a resume.' This was to be the beginning of a new and fascinating career path.

God has a way of redirecting us when we drift off our prescribed course and clearly there was some reason I was being led back into teaching, albeit from a new angle. I didn't really have a clue what I was in for, but my new employer had chosen me, and I was determined to give it all my energy. My adult students were a diverse mix of characters and backgrounds with one common status; they were all unemployed with no immediate prospects. Their reasons for this were varied but, for many, school had not served them well and they had abandoned that institution without qualifications, or any clear idea of their options. It was possible, even likely, that some of them may have been undiagnosed dyslexics who had not been supported at school and had lost confidence in their ability to achieve anything worthwhile.

The learning goals for my programme were appropriately described as Learning and Life Skills. Some were as basic as what to wear to a job interview. I recall learning one of my students had turned up at a local warehouse for his interview wearing a sweatshirt, beach shorts, and gumboots! The wardrobe of the unemployed tended to be minimalist so a unit on appropriate interview clothing was immediately incorporated into the programme and included a visit to a well-stocked second-hand clothing warehouse.

My new career path accelerated from here on with my role as a teacher of life skills expanding to include retail and customer services, office administration skills and English literacy. A certificate in adult teaching led to a graduate diploma and ultimately a degree in education. As my confidence ascended to new heights, I set my sights a little higher and before too long I was working in a government funded agency contract-managing programme approvals for tertiary education providers, such as those I had previously worked for, and facilitating training for teachers of adult learners, with a focus on improving literacy and numeracy competencies. Wearing my new hat as a Literacy Advisor, I was enjoying a role with variety and a certain degree of autonomy which included regular and interesting diversions in the form of trips away to meetings, conferences and seminars. My job satisfaction level rating was rising rapidly, I finally felt I had arrived.

I recall being told that the only certainty in life is change. One requirement for this work was the ability to work under pressure. Funnily enough I found time pressure stimulating and had no difficulty focusing on any task with urgency; it was change that caused me the most angst. Restructuring is a familiar element in any government funded body and, during a very happy tenure with this organisation, I survived two. After nine and a half years the third one knocked this bird completely off her comfortable perch!

At this point the pathway became rocky both personally and career wise. Within a space of a few months, I discovered my husband had been behaving badly with another woman, my mother had just been diagnosed with a terminal illness, and I had been restructured into a role that I found less than inspiring, not least of all because it was predominantly desk-based; it was time to review my options.

With my almost 15-year-old daughter, I left our beautiful island home, moved south to be closer to Mum and took up a six-month contract as a teacher's assistant in a nearby secondary school. This provided me with firsthand insights into the fallibilities of the school system, especially regarding its support, or lack of, for students with learning difficulties. There was a specialist department, but it soon became evident to me that it was not only under resourced but regarded as being of a lesser status within the school. I was shocked how compartmentalised and prejudiced the school system had become, or perhaps it was always so, and I simply hadn't noticed.

My special interest in Dyslexia led me to attend a one-week course but when I suggested sharing some of my learnings with other staff I was fobbed off, that was the job of the SENCO (special education needs coordinator). After all I must not forget that I was only employed as a lowly Teachers' Assistant! The irony was that I was equally well, or perhaps more, qualified and experienced than many of the teaching staff there, especially in the field of literacy.

Meanwhile, my mother, who had been doing well, suffered a sudden decline which culminated in a week-long hospital stay from which she did not ultimately recover. We had all been at her bedside for a week and it was a horrid time. Our father was understandably bereft. As the eldest it fell on me to organise the funeral and, with some support from my three siblings, help him through the adjustment. With Mum gone it must have been lonely out at the farm with only two cats for company, but he never complained and expressed no desire to move. Farm life had framed his life view since childhood; it was where he felt most comfortable. We visited most days and took turns taking him shopping, his once weekly outing. Tragically, three months later, our father suffered a serious stroke which saw us once again camping together in the hospital. When, about six days later, he finally slipped quietly away he was surrounded by his four children, and nine grandchildren.

At the conclusion of my six-month contract as a Teaching Assistant, I jumped off that bus willingly and set my sights on a new role more closely aligned with my passions and qualifications. For the next four years I held a specialist role in a tertiary institute, supporting staff with strategies to improve students' literacy and numeracy skills. During this time, I also completed another degree, specialising in literacy and numeracy with older learners. The principle we were promoting and modelling to teaching staff was that, as language is the foundation of all teaching and learning, every teacher, whatever their specialist area, is a teacher of the English language. Under the term 'contextual literacy', we led them to identify and explore the foundational literacy and numeracy knowledge fundamental to their subject area and plan to explicitly teach this knowledge. This I view as a critical skill lacking in most of our secondary and tertiary educators; literacy and numeracy skills are weak in so many of our students. For most of these tertiary teachers their curriculum is quite specialised; they believed teaching literacy was the job of primary schools. Amongst them I discovered prejudice and resistance to change. "I don't need this! I've been teaching for forty years, why do I need to change?". The old school ways were so embedded, no wonder we still had a literacy problem! Recently when I encountered a similar attitude, I considered that it is more likely a result of a fear of being judged for their lack of knowledge. This lack of knowledge is not their fault; teachers have never been adequately prepared or equipped to support the learning 'challenged'. This needs to change.

Four years on, restructuring and government funding reductions saw an end to this role too and my alternative education research role, although interesting, was only part-time pay but with full-time expectations! Once again, I was re-thinking my career path.

Chapter Thirteen

Embracing the Roadblock

> *Be brave. Take risks.*
> *Nothing can substitute experience.*
> *Paulo Coelho*

For my entire adult life Dyslexia has been like an oddly shaped rock in my path that I keep tripping over, before kicking it away into the 'too hard basket'. It was time I took hold of this rock and found a way to manage it, to work with it purposefully and productively.

In 2009 I tripped over, or rather danced into, a dyslexic someone who later became an encouraging ray of sunshine in my so far rather discombobulated life. Our relationship was a slow development; history tends to repeat, and I had learned to distrust my choices in male friends. When he revealed his dyslexic self to me, I shared my special interest in the condition, and I was thrilled when he encouraged me to progress my ideas. The concept of the Tiri Learning Café was still just a seed, but it was beginning to sprout.

In 2014, I undertook a small-scale investigation by way of a needs analysis. I conducted my inquiry across several local primary and intermediate schools and met with principals and deputy principals in six local schools. I discovered that few teachers, and even fewer school leaders, had any practical understanding of Dyslexia, or any learning difficulties. Some schools allowed external specialists to conduct targeted literacy intervention sessions for students with a professionally diagnosed learning difficulty; these tutors were not employed by the school but paid by the parents, who were not even observers of the sessions, and apparently nothing was shared with their class teachers.

It was during these investigations that I met another researcher who was examining the school experiences of students with ADHD. It was she who alerted me to the comorbidity of ADHD and Dyslexia; her findings indicated that, in as many as 40% of ADHD children she had encountered, Dyslexia was also a factor.

I became aware that there were significant misunderstandings about both conditions. ADHD was mostly considered a problem found only in boys. The most popular view was that it was a behavioural problem that should be addressed through firm behaviour management, or positive re-enforcement strategies. Understanding, as I do now, how emotionally sensitive the ADHD brain can be, I imagine the disciplinary responses created more angst than they averted.

Early assessments of Dyslexia (Berlin, 1883, and Kussmaul, 1877) identified Dyslexia as a brain-based disease affecting reading; from these studies the term 'word blindness' evolved. Some have theorised that 'Dyslexia' was a temporary condition that could be 'cured' with the right programme, but most specialists now agree that this is false. The Rose Report (2009) provided a useful working definition, describing it as 'a learning difficulty that primarily affects the skills involved in accurate and fluent word reading and spelling, presenting as 'difficulties in phonological awareness, verbal memory and verbal processing speed. Although the arguments continue, with some radically suggesting that the term Dyslexia was fabricated by the wealthy class, eminent scholars and proclaimed experts of the twentieth century and beyond generally agree that Dyslexia is a recognisable and identifiable condition that 'occurs across the range of intellectual abilities.

Misunderstandings and myths about Dyslexia have led parents to waste time and money chasing the magic cure for their child's disability. An ex-work colleague, Geraldine, whose son had been diagnosed with Dyslexia, had been desperately chasing such a cure for a year or more when I met them. Geraldine had tried multiple 'treatments', including the Irlen's lenses, coloured paper overlays, a couple of alternative educational programmes and some specific and very expensive audio accessories which her son hated and refused to use. Her most extreme choice was the Arrowsmith programme, a specially designed and very expensive immersion programme that claimed to "change brains and transform lives" via an approach described as 'cognitive enhancement'. Not only were these changes unsettling for her son but they did not help him with his learning difficulties. Ultimately, she was forced to realise that none of this alleviated her son's difficulties and there was no magic bullet. She did report an immediate improvement when she reverted to the 1-1 tutoring approach she had started with.

It was around this time that the idea of Tiri Language and Literacy was conceived.

Chapter Fourteen

An Idea is Born

> *Making a decision was only the beginning of things. When someone makes a decision, he is really diving into a strong current that will carry him to places he had never dreamed of when he first made the decision.*
> Paulo Coelho

During 2015 a lot changed in my personal life. My daughter was settled in a new home with her soon-to-be husband and one child, my country house was rented, and I had made a life commitment to my dancing dyslexic friend. Later that year, fed up with restructures and redundancies and motivated by the potential for better work opportunities and family reconnections, we packed our belongings and left the Land of the Long White Cloud to relocate to Western Australia. The story of that exciting but exhausting transition is part of another, yet-to-be-completed book.

As with any move, there were many stresses and uncertainties, but we persevered: in June 2016, we had established ourselves in our semi-rural home south of Perth. Our sprawling five-bedroom house sits on a tranquil five acres of remnant coastal forest, a mixed woodland of Marri, Banksia, and Jarrah. This spacious home, with its enormous entertainment room, has enabled me to finally fulfil my long-held dream to establish my own learning zone where I could provide specialist individualised teaching and support for children with Dyslexia.

Getting started did require making some connections, something we, as very recent immigrants to Perth, did not have in abundance. Earlier that year, I had stumbled upon the Dyslexia SPELD Foundation (DSF) in Perth and enrolled on several workshops and professional development courses. As a professional member of DSF I was registered on their website, and this is how I found my first students, or rather, they found me.

The most valuable of all the workshops was an intensive two-week training programme teaching a relatively new phonics approach known as Sounds Write (Walker & Co.). I immediately fell in love with the simplicity of this programme. In the development of this programme, Walker was inspired by Diane McGuiness's book 'Linguistic Phonics'. The syllabus follows a Systematic Synthetic Phonics approach. Synthetic does not in this instance mean 'artificial' or 'fake' but is reference to the way the various elements of this phonics programme are carefully 'synthesised', or fused, to teach, explicitly, the alphabetic code knowledge in a logical progressive sequence.

The typical dyslexic finds learning to read and write an exhaustive and tedious process, but I discovered how well the logical sequencing of this programme, along with the built-in revisions and repetitions, made the whole process of reading and writing more attainable for these young dyslexic students. It works especially well for the young beginning readers (6-8 years) with whom I have witnessed significant gains almost immediately.

Finally, I had found the programme that, enhanced by my deepened understanding of the neurodiverse brain, would equip me with the skills and knowledge to provide effective literacy interventions for struggling readers and writers, such as those with Dyslexia, and ADHD. What I now needed was a strategic framework that ensured every child under my tutelage had the best opportunity to become a successful reader and writer.

An Idea is Born

I had been hatching a plan, a 'construct' which places the child at the centre of a supportive web of informed 'others', individuals who are already, personally, professionally, or socially, supporting and influencing his/her development.

My conceptual creation, Tiri Language & Literacy, was resurrected from old dreams and nourished by new knowledge and ideas. Tiri comes from the name of the NZ street we lived in before moving to Western Australia. In Māori, the language of the indigenous people of New Zealand, *Tiri* means to plant or sow (seeds, crops, etc.), which seems to me a highly appropriate analogy for what we are doing here.

I am teaching the fundamentals of reading and writing in much the same way that a music teacher teaches the relationship between musical notation and the sounds produced on their instrument. As we teach the alphabetic code, we are planting seeds of knowledge and spawning an increasingly comprehensive understanding of the English language and how the pieces fit together. Once the student can decipher the code, they are equipped to read and learn independently. I have been, and continue to be, inspired by the results of this approach. When we sow strong, healthy seeds of reading knowledge, and practise well and often, ultimately what grows is a competent and confident reader who begins to enjoy books and the stories they share.

The Tiri philosophy places the child at the centre. Like a seedling in a forest, the child is supported as they develop their literacy skills and knowledge at their own pace without the pressures of time or performance expectations, or the discomfort of comparing themselves to others. The 'wrap-around' approach is designed explicitly to support the neurodiverse child to maintain healthy self-esteem and build confidence as they face their difficulties head-on. Protected by the supporting layers above and around them (parent(s), family, school, classroom teacher, and specialist teacher) they are fed, nurtured, and encouraged as they build their skills. A child with learning difficulties is acutely aware of their deficiencies and constantly measures themselves against their peers. Anxiety and even depression are too common amongst these children, particularly when they are undiagnosed and unsupported.

In my programme, parent commitment to the process is crucial and parent attendance at our sessions is mandatory. For the initial sessions, particularly, I share the foundational theories and methodologies with the parents, so they understand how to lead their child through their home practice activities. For a child with learning difficulties who has fallen well behind his/her peers, one hour per week is never sufficient to improve their situation at a significant rate; the longer it takes, the further behind they fall and the greater the likelihood of it impacting negatively on their mental health. I am confident that my individualised, one-to-one approach is the most appropriate for these children; it enables them to address their specific learning deficits without feeling the shame that comes from being exposed as the only one of a group or class that is unable to read or write to the level of his/her peers. School is at the best of times a competitive environment and in the quest to defer attention from their own perceived inadequacies, children can be judgmental and cruel.

Of course, this individualised teaching incurs an extra cost and time commitment for the parents because most schools cannot provide the level of literacy intervention required. One session per week is the standard, but even when one catches them in their first or second year of schooling this one hour can never be enough to make up their deficits, they need daily and repeated practice. For a dyslexic child for whom learning to read has thus far seemed a near impossible task that child's progress is directly commensurate with the quantity and quality of the follow-up practice during the week, and this falls upon the parents. Preparing and training the parents for this is an essential and cumulative component of my programme.

Regular and repeated practice framed in a familiar format builds confidence and consolidates the learning; when, as sometimes happens, we get buy-in from their class teacher, some collaboration is possible, and that child's progress accelerates. When I sense that the practice regime is not being followed at home, I am concerned – there is no place for complacency when a child is helplessly floundering in a swamp of confusion about their abilities in a skill that is fundamental to their life now, and in the future.

Whilst I am passionately committed to my philosophy, especially to the wrap-around approach, I accept that it is not possible to implement it perfectly in every case. With the diversity of knowledge and attitudes, and varied understandings within and between schools and teachers, not to mention the hotly contested arguments about how we should be teaching children to read and write, we cannot achieve a complete 'wrap' for all. I am hopeful that, as The Science of Reading message spreads, this situation will eventually change.

You may have heard of 'The Reading Wars'. Nationally and internationally, the debates regarding the best methods for teaching reading have raged into a furious war between two leading contestants, 'Phonics' and 'Whole Language'. The 'Whole Language' approach, which became popular in the 1980s, is founded on the belief that learning to read, write and spell are innate and natural abilities. It is the hotly argued thesis of the Whole Language proponents that we simply need to immerse children in books, and they will naturally learn to read. This principle is certainly true of oral language skills, but I have yet to see any evidence that this applies to reading and writing. I believe their theory is a misguided fabrication. Reflecting on my music learning analogy, simply listening to a piece of music, no matter how many times we hear it, will not teach us to interpret the musical notations on the song sheet. We cannot learn these practical skills by osmosis. The Whole Language approach teaches young readers to use context and picture clues to decipher more challenging words, then commit those new words to memory. The load on the working memory grows exponentially heavier with every reading level and, without the foundational knowledge that phonics provides, numerous early learners struggle, and many are left far behind. Many of these will leave school as statistical failures, but this is not necessary.

Whilst the Reading Wars continue, I am encouraged by mounting support for the use of phonics in early reading instruction, particularly because I know this method is a game changer, not only for dyslexics. There are varying degrees of commitment with many schools still opting for a 'Balanced Literacy' programme, what I view as a contrived mixture of phonics and 'Whole Language' teaching strategies. With a balanced literacy approach, phonics is applied to some spelling instruction, but there is little structure or fusion in the application. The whole language principles continue to predominate, which can be especially confusing for learners with working memory challenges.

Mixing the menu in this way, I believe, leads to a watering down of the phonics component. Instead, we get literacy instruction that is somewhat random, unstructured and *far from* synthesised, with the potential for confusion, especially for those who struggle with reading and writing. A well-designed phonics programme, with a synthesised and systematic approach, enriched by the explicit inclusion of relevant morphology, enables children to build literacy knowledge and skills in a logically connected manner, whilst enhancing comprehension and spelling. Sounds Write is certainly not the only one, but it is my current favourite phonics programme because it has proven effective and simple to implement. The progressive layering of skills provides multiple opportunities for revision and practice of this knowledge whilst they build new knowledge. This repetition is essential for a dyslexic child especially.

In his book *Right-Brained Children in a Left-Brained World*, Freed (1998) suggests there are some for whom phonics makes no sense. Whilst I appreciate what Freed says about those he describes as 'right-brained' and am open to considering there may be other methods we can employ to support these children to learn to read and write, I am still convinced that structured synthetic phonics is the most thoroughly effective system to teach them by. From my experience, for any young child beginning their literacy journey, phonics is the most effective strategy to launch and build solid literacy skills. For a child with Dyslexia anything other than phonics is a fast track to failure. Learning to read and spell is never easy for them, especially those diagnosed with 'severe' Dyslexia, but phonics provides a solid reference point.

When you teach the mechanics of the language, that is the alphabet code, you are not only teaching reading and writing skills but also revealing, bit by bit, how the code works. Progressively, our developing readers and writers can use that knowledge to read and spell more complex words. Whilst important, code knowledge alone is not enough; as their skills build, it is crucial that we concurrently introduce the relevant syntax, semantics, and morphology to strengthen these foundations. When we expose them to model texts and provide multiple opportunities to practice in a supported setting these students can become good writers too

How important is a diagnosis? Whilst a diagnosis does not alter the needs of the child, it does achieve at least two important objectives. A diagnosis can return a child's self-respect as he/she learns that he/she is not stupid but that there is a neurological cause for their difficulties, a reason beyond their control. A diagnosis also serves as a lever for the furiously advocating parent trying to get the supportive *'accommodations'* and *adjustments* their child needs in the classroom.

The earlier we can establish a diagnosis the more quickly we can address a child's specific learning challenges and prevent further slippage, mentally, and emotionally as well as academically. Unfortunately, in Australia, the cost of this process is financially significant and can be prohibitive to many families. Whilst schools are expected to meet the needs of all their students whether their learning disability is imputed or confirmed by diagnosis, I am aware that this is not always the case. Special accommodations for formal examinations or assessments require professional diagnosis before they can be approved. Whilst an official diagnosis and its accompanying report educate and empower parents to become proactive advocates for their child, currently, there is no financial support for a Dyslexia assessment, and many are never diagnosed.

Parent advocacy can be an exhausting and time-consuming endeavour, and one not all parents are confident to undertake without some coaching. I find it slightly disturbing that this is now becoming a business opportunity, an additional cost for parents who are already unfairly disadvantaged because schools and teachers are inadequately resourced.

For each of my intervention students, I develop an individualised plan, which is reviewed term by term. This plan, and my semester report, is shared with parents, and I encourage them to also share it with their child's teacher. Many teachers are happy to integrate some of my recommendations, for example adjusting the child's spelling targets, which not only reduces their mental and emotional stress, but the complementary approach also helps consolidate the skills we are working on. Each session I take is tailored specifically to meet the current learning needs of the child, being mindful of their strengths, weaknesses, and special interests. There is no set timeframe for completing any stage of the programme and it is understood that 'completion' does not mean automaticity. Repeated practice is critical to consolidating learning and making sustainable progress and with everything they have invested in this, parents are encouraged to take responsibility for driving this ship forward.

In an ideal world this specialist intervention should be provided and scheduled within a child's school day, and embedded in the context of their various subjects, but I am not aware of any school that is yet equipped to do this effectively, many not at all. If miracles happen and this situation reverses, I will be out of a job but entirely delighted to know that our children with learning difficulties such as Dyslexia and ADHD, will no longer be so disadvantaged at school.

Chapter Fifteen

ADHD, the child Misunderstood

> There is only one thing that makes a dream impossible to achieve: the fear of failure.
> Paulo Coelho

For many of my intervention students, Dyslexia is not their sole issue; within my current cohort 30% also have an ADHD diagnosis. This is in line with statistical information that tells us between 25% and 40% of children with Dyslexia also have ADHD. These two disorders share several characteristics, which can complicate the diagnostic process as well as the management of each condition. Like Dyslexia, ADHD creates difficulties with learning, but this is due to their difficulties maintaining attention and focus, while for the dyslexic their concentration is challenged because reading is such an effort for them that mental exhaustion leaves them depleted.

The human brain is the control centre for all our bodily functions and movement, including our thoughts, memory, and emotions. Essentially all human brains conform to the same structural pattern, but no two are identical in every aspect. Whilst many people's brains are similar enough for them not to be labelled, there will always be variations between individuals. This is known as 'neurodiversity'. Many brain differences are barely perceptible, while others are obvious, even to the untrained. Parents know their children best and often notice something is amiss before their teachers. Brain differences such as Dyslexia and attention-deficit-hyperactivity disorder (ADHD) are two of the most commonly identifiable 'neurodivergent' brain types, but without explicit training, many teachers may be unaware of them.

Conservatively, it is estimated that as many as 20% of our population is affected by these conditions; however, these statistics are unreliable because, usually for financial reasons, many are never formally diagnosed. Each of these conditions has by many been termed 'a disability' because they are seen to cause a disadvantage for the individual, particularly in the school environment. For the dyslexic brain, especially, it is predominantly in the realm of reading and writing that their 'disability' fully emerges. Often the first time this becomes evident is when a child begins their formal schooling.

With ADHD also it is usually in the school setting that their behaviours are recognised as unusual. Most young children are naturally active and curious and have limited capacity for sitting still, as is expected for the traditional 'mat time' sessions, but the overstimulated ADHD brain is almost incapable of this. In this highly structured and standardised setting, which is designed to cater for the neurotypical, every neurodivergent brain struggles, and generally fails, to appear 'normal'. Who wants to be *normal*, one might ask. Normal is ordinary, uninteresting, blending in, yet normal reaps the greatest rewards at school. Being different can be difficult, but it should not be considered a disability.

As with Dyslexia, it is often only in the classroom setting that the differences of the ADHD brain become significant. Sitting still and quietly for sustained periods, listening to and following instructions, focusing on a task to completion; these are unnatural to the ADHD child. For the child who tries but fails to fit in, normal seems desirable, it is what they constantly aspire to but never achieve. As the atypical child battles their difficulties, their differences magnify and many negative thoughts can lead to negative behaviours, low self-esteem, lack of confidence, anxiety, and possibly depression. Recognising the potential impact on mental wellbeing, it is not surprising to discover how significant Dyslexia, and ADHD, is amongst prison inmates, and easy to understand how the consequence of ignoring their early struggles may have led them to this outcome. (Lashlie, 2002).

As I work with and learn more about these two conditions, and reflect upon my own school learning struggles, I realise how closely my experiences reflect those of many of my students. At that time, I did not understand the reasons behind my difficulties, and I frequently felt I was *stupid*. The associated expectation of failure and intense fear of being identified as such led me to avoid or give up many pursuits without effectively testing that belief. If you do not try, you cannot fail.

Representatives of the neurodivergent ADHD brain type are found in every classroom in every school. It has long been a common misconception that ADHD is a condition predominantly found in boys and that it manifests in disturbing physical behaviours, a fact that has left many ADHD girls unrecognised and undiagnosed. More recent research suggests that ADHD, like Dyslexia, is passed genetically through families, and that it occurs in both boys and girls. If you or anyone in your immediate family has ADHD, it may serve you well to research your ancestry and watch your children for signs.

Gabor Maté (1999) has some other fascinating and highly plausible ideas about the origins of ADHD, for which I give more detail in Chapter 20. I highly recommend his book, *Scattered Minds*.

ADHD may present in various ways, but there are some identifiable traits shared by most individuals. Dr Barkley (2013) suggests that ADHD is a misleading title. He describes ADHD as a condition of executive dysfunction, with three key features: emotional dysregulation, inattentiveness, and time blindness. The area of the brain responsible for emotional regulation tends to develop more slowly than it does in their non-ADHD peers, leaving them as many as two or three years behind. They tend to act and react impulsively, expressing their feelings both audibly and physically without considering the consequences, speaking their thoughts without fully thinking them through. Within the ADHD brain there can be an almost constant dialogue of thoughts and visualisations which intercept and interfere with their ability to concentrate on the task to hand. Their chronic distractibility leads to careless mistakes, tasks incomplete, or not even started. Whilst attempting to organise ideas and decide how to begin what seems an impossible task, time simply evaporates. This sounds very much like me during my school days.

Inattentiveness and distractibility are significant handicaps to the ADHD brain. Despite my heightened understanding, these continue to challenge me daily. I have developed a few strategies to improve my time management, such as alarms, lists, and odd visual reminders. Thank goodness maturity has had a positive influence on my emotional regulation! With a brain that is managing a million thoughts in a short time the stress on the working memory is unimaginable. No wonder your ADHD friend appears frenetic at times; with such a busy mind it is difficult for them to be still for long, they can be exhausting companions.

It is generally agreed that ADHD is a neurodevelopmental disorder which, according to statistics available from ADHD Australia, affects approximately 281,200 children and adolescents (0-19 years old) and 533,300 adults in Australia.

It is estimated there is at least one child with ADHD in every classroom. How sad then that so many teachers lack the knowledge and understanding to enable them to recognise and effectively support these children.

It has been established that ADHD is neurological in origin, possibly more accurately described as an 'Executive Functioning' disorder, characterised by noticeable challenges with time management, planning and emotional regulation. (Barkley, 2016, and Brown, 2018). The habitual procrastination I witnessed in my mother has been identified as a common problem for the ADHD individual, and I, too, am a classic offender! Why? Is it laziness? Joseph Ferrari (2010) concludes that procrastination has nothing to do with organisation or time management but stems from an inherent inability to effectively regulate our emotions and make decisions. When our choices are multiple and poorly defined, overwhelm steps in and freezes us in a state of indecision.

The 'attention deficit' aspect is somewhat misleading. It is not impossible for the ADHD brain to pay attention, especially if the activity is of special interest. The challenges to attention are largely three-fold, giving attention to activities that do not interest you, maintaining attention when faced with distractions, and hyper-attentiveness when absorbed in an especially engaging and enjoyable activity. Changing activities, especially when that task is incomplete, can cause the ADHD child considerable angst, sometimes leading to meltdowns. This can be reduced when one gives them plenty of time to consider, accept, and prepare for the change.

For the older ADHD too, being required to change focus without completing something can create additional mental and emotional discomfort. Collecting and organising multiple ideas and coordinating different pieces of information as one does for an essay or report requires intense concentration, something the ADHD brain finds difficult enough. Interruptions that break an already tenuous link with mindful attention can mean having to start again. This was one of the aspects of secondary school that I struggled with enormously; every 50 minutes the bell rang and suddenly we had to break concentration and move on to the next activity, usually at a different location. Any new information, knowledge or great ideas in the making were inconveniently wiped from my memory!

As a teacher, I am privileged to be able to apply my lived experience and newly honed understanding of the quaint and unpredictable ADHD brain. I can appreciate and relate to the challenges many of my students may face in their personal journeys. In this, my lifelong struggle has been to some (altruistic) purpose. However, whilst my personal experience has built valuable knowledge and understanding of the many outward features of both Dyslexia and ADHD, it has taken years of inquiry, reading, investigations, and university studies to be able to finally 'connect the dots' and make tangible sense of it all.

In a recent Australian survey, many teachers admitted they do not know how to help students with ADHD (ADHD Australia, 2021). Some said they felt confident enough to recognise those children in their classroom but did not feel adequately prepared with strategies that they can employ to help their ADHD students. As I have mentioned, ADHD frequently co-occurs with other disorders, such as Dyslexia, Dysgraphia, and Autism, which may mask or delay the diagnosis of ADHD. Dyslexia too remains a mystery to many teachers, for some their awareness being limited to the name alone and others thinking it is simply a problem with letter reversals.

Apart from those who major in Special Education, it seems that student teachers generally receive no special training in teaching the neurodiverse. In a recent social media chat, one teacher candidly revealed that her initial teacher training provided no help regarding this. This is an unacceptable oversight when we know these children make up a conservatively estimated 20% of school enrolments. School curriculum guides from most state education authorities contain a section listing acceptable classroom adjustments they might employ for these children, but what I have observed is that the application of these is inconsistent between, and even within, schools and, frustratingly, few teachers are adequately equipped or supported with this.

One of three key areas of concern from the 2020 survey into 'community gaps and priorities' (ADHD Australia, 2020) was that teachers need to be able to accommodate, empathise with and understand the unique challenges faced by ADHD children and how to help them. Undeniably the same concerns apply in the case of the commonly co-occurring condition, Dyslexia. To do this effectively our teachers require some specific knowledge and understanding. At a minimum they should have:

- Knowledge of how ADHD (& Dyslexia) may present so they can recognise it,
- Understanding regarding how to respond to and work with these students,
- Knowledge of and familiarity with the appropriate 'accommodations', and adjustments and how they can apply these,

- Awareness of and access to supportive resources, including training.

Additionally, schools need the infrastructure to ensure the effective implementation of these understandings.

Chapter Sixteen

The Dyslexic Disadvantage

The world has a soul and whoever understands that soul can also understand the language of many things.
Paulo Coelho

Being able to read and write is not just fundamental to managing our daily lives, but a critical ability for all learning. Reading is the pathway to knowledge and our poor readers are disadvantaged. In the early centuries, only the wealthy had access to education and, until the early 18th century, it was only for boys. Even today discriminatory practices in many countries prevent females from accessing learning on the same basis as males. (UNESCO, 2024). Here in the Asia Pacific region, we are privileged, education is not only freely available to all, but legislation decrees that every child, regardless of race, or socio-economic status, has the right to learn to read and write. Well, that is the intent.

If we look back far enough, we can find the foundations of our current education system have been attributed to Saint Augustine, an early Christian theologian and philosopher in Medieval times. Augustine is not only credited with founding Kings School in Canterbury, England, but was also a prolific author. In those very early days (c400-600AD) schools were exclusively church owned and managed, and their curriculum was limited to Latin, the language of the Bible, and prepared boys for religious service such as singing in the choir. Today, churches continue to be major contributors to education, but whilst their curriculum has extended to include much more than religious studies, most church schools follow a similar model and are managed outside the jurisdiction of the state authorities.

Our contemporary schools exist in many different shapes and sizes but, disappointingly, despite a small degree of flexibility between them, most choose to model themselves upon the same fundamental design, curriculum, and philosophy, the one-size-fits-all approach. Since we clearly have such diversity amongst our populace, and so many students failing, why do most schools continue to teach by the same recipe? Imagine if every restaurant offered the same menu!

In my experience, the current education system is persistently failing to meet the needs of a significant proportion of our population. Is this through ignorance, poor management, or misdirected priorities? Many of us know at least one of these children. If you are a teacher, you may also know the frustration from the lack of resources to equitably serve the diverse needs you see in your classroom. Most children I work with have been poorly served by their school. This is not the fault of teachers who are, for the most part, time and resource-poor. This realisation fuels my view that our highly prescriptive and largely authoritarian establishment lacks any genuine sense of connection with the community it supposedly serves.

One of the most restrictive control mechanisms of the school education system is the grouping of children in chronological age groups. How and why has this system been adopted? Is it based upon a misguided belief that all children should develop and learn at a similar rate, or is it designed to build a society of conformists? I believe this system works for almost nobody! But it especially fails many of our otherwise capable and creative children who, because of a neurological brain difference such as Dyslexia, or a developmental difference such as ADHD, find learning to read and write more difficult than others. For those seriously impacted by ADHD the differences in their executive functioning capabilities are heightened in a single age-group classroom. The tardiness of their emotional development (potentially as many as three years behind) leaves them struggling socially, and emotionally. They feel inadequate; their brains *do* work differently but they are not mentally disabled. The other school restriction that creates misery for many is the imposed curriculum, for example the compulsory requirement for some to study a second language creates unnecessary additional stress, particularly for the dyslexic who is still grappling with their first.

Whilst some labels may be considered limiting, a confirmed diagnosis such as Dyslexia or ADHD, or both, can be empowering, inspiring new hope to students and their parents. Understanding that their brain is not broken but works differently; learning that, with appropriate strategies and approaches they can succeed, is transformational.

For many children, including me, starting primary school is an eagerly awaited event. For many neurodiverse children, school is where their happy-go-lucky lives end, and the anxieties begin. From day one the focus is on the exciting journey towards becoming a reader and writer, but it doesn't take long for the performance challenges to become apparent and the initial enthusiasm to be replaced by apprehension.

Dyslexia and ADHD are common to every classroom, but schools are not known for their flexibility and most teachers have not been trained to recognise, understand, and accommodate the variable learning needs of these children. They do not know that trying harder, staying in at lunchtime, or completing extra homework will not help and will only serve to intensify their anxieties and negative feelings. However, for many teachers, these are the only options they have in their toolbox. Being 'different' is generally seen as a problem rather than an opportunity, with the emphasis predominantly on training the child to 'fit' the system. Children quickly pick up on others' weaknesses, and in the somewhat competitive environment of school, these differently wired children often suffer hurtful judgments. For the neurodiverse child, this too commonly leads to a loss of confidence, poor self-esteem, and increasing anxiety when faced with reading and writing tasks. Avoidance is a popular and understandable strategy. At reading time, a young boy who admits that reading is something he would rather not do, always has an important question that needs answering, or a story he needs to share. These distractions are merely strategies to disguise his shattered self-belief and delay the inevitable shame.

One of my young students came to me at age 6 and a half years. After six months in Pre-primary (kindergarten) and two terms in Year One, this bright and articulate boy was almost entirely illiterate. At his second session his mother told me that he had asked her why she was wasting time taking him to reading classes; he believed I wouldn't be able to teach him to read because he was 'dumb'. He had already come to accept his inadequacy as a lack of ability, a concept which had been reinforced by his teacher and his peers. For those first months his anxiety was ever-present, with frequent toilet visits and regular stomach complaints. Almost four years later his anxiety level is noticeably reduced and his reading and writing skills and knowledge have grown so rapidly that he has been forced to revise his opinion. Whilst acknowledging the critical importance of developing good literacy skills, we must not overlook the value of artistic pursuits. The opportunity for creative expression can be a powerful contributor to a healthy mind. Not only do such activities offer respite from the more tightly managed classroom instruction but provide an avenue for expressing and releasing inner frustrations. Many neurodiverse children I know demonstrate quite exceptional talent for one or more of the arts and success in this field can positively impact all areas of their development. Maté (1999) suggests that art and music are equally important as literacy and numeracy, and I agree. Not only are these potential areas of individual talent but music is known to help the ADHD brain regulate, and as I have experienced, it can improve attention and focus.

A parent may not be familiar with Dyslexia, but they will recognise the mismatch between their child's apparently quick and agile mind and their reported slow progress at school. The child will usually judge themselves against others and, no matter how encouraging their parents, that child will know they are failing to meet expectations.

Obtaining a diagnosis is important, and the earlier the better. Once a child realises there is a physiological reason for their 'difference' and that they are not stupid or unintelligent, their feelings of shame can be replaced by hopefulness, and their parents' torment turned to relief and understanding. Tragically, the cost of a professional diagnosis can be prohibitive for some families, and this cost may increase where there is more than one issue, such as Dyslexia *and* ADHD, where two assessments are required. However, the diagnosis is not the only important change needed to improve their self-view. For most children, school is a major part of their lives, and this is commonly the place where differences such as ADHD and Dyslexia cause the greatest angst. The ability to read is our ticket to learning, our passport to the world. Knowledge is powerful, and much of our knowledge is acquired through reading; the disadvantage of poor literacy is immeasurable.

More knowledge and understanding amongst our teachers is crucial; how can they enable and empower these neurodiverse children to discover their potential, improve their schooling experience and their achievements? Our teachers are doing their best, but it is not yet enough.

Maté (1999) developed a set of guidelines to help teachers with ADHD children in the classroom. I have summarised them here because I think they are helpful and practical; I think these principles can be usefully applied in all teaching situations, but especially with neurodivergent children such as those with Dyslexia and ADHD.

- Maintain the fundamental principle, **do no harm**. Avoid any action that is likely to cause that child emotional pain, such as public criticism, and comparisons to others.
- Build a strong working relationship with **the parents** with the goal of sharing the challenges in a mutually supportive way.
- **Build a relationship of trust** with the child. Focus on building an honest mutually rewarding relationship that is beneficial to you as well as the child. Take time to learn about them, their unique behaviours, needs, interests. Learn about and apply any supportive strategies.
- **Facilitate opportunities** for creative and unstructured time away from the classroom if possible (e.g. music, art, sport).
- **Adjust** your **academic expectations** and consider only what specifically is being assessed. Be aware of the extra stress and anxiety caused by time restrictions and take all precautions to avoid this.

Chapter Seventeen

ADHD, an Emotional Powerhouse

> *In order for us to liberate the energy of our strength, our weakness must first have a chance to reveal itself.*
> *Paulo Coelho*

Officially, there are three, professionally recognised, diagnostic types of ADHD (DSM-5). These are:

1. Predominantly hyperactive/impulsive
2. Predominantly inattentive type
3. Combined hyperactive/impulsive/inattentive.

Underlying each of these types are difficulties with the executive functions responsible for planning and time management, as well as emotional self-regulation. The executive functioning of children with ADHD may operate at an emotional level as many as three years behind that expected at their chronological age. Much like Autism, ADHD is a spectrum disorder (Brown, 2018) in that there is noticeable variability in the levels of impairment from mild to moderate or severe. As Barkley (2016) explains, this is essentially a developmental delay rather than a permanent functional impairment.

A common misconception is that ADHD is predominantly found in boys, this is most likely because girls tend to present their ADHD differently. A greater number of girls are diagnosed with the predominantly inattentive type, but hyperactivity is often there too. One clue may be their constant fidgeting, or stimming, combined with an inability to sit still for long. Stimming is a common, but not exclusive, trait of the neurodiverse, seen particularly in ADHD and ASD individuals. Stimming is a repetitive, self-stimulating activity that may involve one or many senses; some examples are body movements such as repeatedly tapping fingers or a pencil on a table, twirling a strand of hair around a finger, biting fingernails, jiggling a leg or foot, knuckle cracking, or doodling. It may also manifest through vocal sounds such as humming, whistling, or tongue clicking, or sensory modes such as touching, holding, feeling, or squeezing a particular item or material.

Hyperactivity may not immediately be recognised because it is not always demonstrated in an outward physical manner but is occurring in the brain with the uncontrollable overload of thoughts. The ADHD brain commonly struggles to concentrate and move sequentially through a project because they are so easily distracted; the sound of a car arriving in the carpark, the sight of a bird flying past the window, or a sudden gust of wind can trigger a diversion that fatally interrupts their attention to a task. The agile yet unpredictable ADHD mind can jump from one thought to another in a matter of moments. Their mental journey may seem logical to them but is entirely confusing to others. I am one of those annoying people who frequently verbalises activities as I work. This strategy helps me stay focused and engaged on more complex tasks but can be extremely disturbing to others nearby.

Whilst most experts view ADHD as an inherited disposition, Gabor Maté (1999) offers us a different perspective. He suggests that ADHD individuals are 'hypersensitive' by nature and that this characteristic renders them susceptible to ADD/ADHD, which he believes is developed as a response to their early experiences. So, we have a naturally sensitive child thrown into a stressful environment, to which their main carer's response is anxiety. This anxiety is picked up and carried by the child. Maté cites his own childhood as an example; when he was a baby and young child Adolf Hitler was leading the persecution of the Jews. Whilst Maté received plenty of love and care, his young Polish mother suffered extreme stress and anxiety due to the ever-present threats of expulsion or imprisonment that were posed to them and other Jewish families at that time. The sensitivity that Maté describes may also manifest in physical allergic reactions. How many ADHD individuals have you met who suffer from hay fever, asthma, or unexplained rashes? I, and each of my siblings, suffered from some or all of these at various times, and our mother too. Maté's conclusions make very good sense to me.

School was always an uncomfortable place for me, as it is for many neurodiverse children. The ADHD child is particularly vulnerable and readily succumbs to poor self-esteem and anxiety. Their anxiety and poor self-image may create difficulties building lasting friendships, for which they will blame themselves.

A common feature of the ADHD brain is its inability to let go of negative memories. When everything is going well the ADHD brain is both stimulated and content, but when things go wrong, they may become so obsessively focused on that issue or situation that they can focus on nothing else, until it is resolved. They tend to believe the issue is their fault and may continually replay the event in their head analysing and re-experiencing it, as they try to understand what went wrong and how they can fix it.

Because of their super sensitivity, criticism, even when it is meant to be constructive, can be difficult for the ADHD to deal with. A teacher's comment can inadvertently lead an ADHD child to wear that criticism as a permanent feature so that they give up trying.

Without training, teachers must be forgiven for misinterpreting the attitudes, misunderstandings, and behaviours of the neurodiverse child in front of them. When fiddling with their hair, twisting the hem of their shirt, wriggling and fidgeting in their chair, or doodling in their book, this child may appear not to be paying any attention to you, or what is happening in the classroom. Teachers may be astonished to learn that what seems like inattention is, more often, the opposite. Constant movement is a hallmark of many individuals with ADHD; their brain is commonly racing like a runaway train and is prone to drifting off focus in moments. Doodling or drawing can be a critical aid to stimulating their attention and maintaining their focus. For a child with Dyslexia, drawing can be an effective way of recording their ideas as they are learning, especially for those who primarily think in pictures. Drawing also removes the stress of writing and can help them more accurately record and reference their learning, rather than be inhibited by their struggle with words.

Whilst it has taken me more than half a lifetime to put a name to it, I realised a long time ago that maintaining concentration has always been, and remains, my number one challenge to completing any project in a reasonable time. My chronic distractibility, along with erratic concentration, remains a constant challenge, and was my greatest enemy at school and beyond. As an adult I have learned to recognise and manage my limitations, but it is a daily battle. My most helpful strategies are my daily planner, alarms to keep me on track, and establishing routines. I always carry a notebook and pencil, and when I am attending to critical information, I will write and draw as I listen; this helps me remain focused.

The increasingly digital age that we live in creates both advantages and disadvantages for brains like mine. There is no doubt in my mind that the digital word processing option would have made completion of my school and earlier university assignments much simpler and undoubtedly saved a bucket-load of paper! On the other hand, it is important to understand the potential negatives of this tool. Keyboarding does not connect to our brains in the same way that physical writing can; being able to scribble my thoughts and ideas on paper and actively check spelling options has always been crucial for my creativity, and for the ultimate completion of written reports and assignments, including this book! For a child with a learning disability, particularly Dyslexia, the physical act of writing, along with the interactive experience of reading and speaking, creates and strengthens the neural pathways in the brain that enable us to become literate. This is especially important during the early learning phase, from kindergarten to year six, when basic literacy skills and knowledge are being built. Using a keyboard instead of handwriting creates a neural disconnect between the reading and the writing process which potentially leads to more effortful writing.

My other great nemesis is my dodgy working memory. Were she still here, my dear mother would absolutely endorse this! Combined with my distractibility and frequent loss of focus, this remains a recurrent challenge for me. It is entirely possible for me to walk over to the bookshelf to retrieve a specific book, on the way there remember that I haven't hung the washing, set out to do that then realise I haven't let the chickens out yet, and while I clean their dishes, I realise I am hungry and go to the kitchen to make lunch, before returning to the work I was doing previously and remember that I needed that book, and, oh darn, the washing still needs hanging! I cannot tell you how many saucepans I have burned because my attention has been diverted in this way! Forgetfulness is common amongst the ADHD cohort. If you need your ADHD child to remember and carry out multiple tasks, try a list, but make it short or they may not even begin. Three is a good number, but for some, just one task at a time is all they can effectively manage. This approach can be a game-changer; most kids will love being able to tick each item as they complete it, and the need for constant reminders will be significantly reduced. For pre-readers, you might use pictures instead.

Planning, prioritising, and creating an organised approach toward specific tasks requires efficient time management and working memory functions, two common deficits of the ADHD brain. Personally, it has been comforting to learn how common this trait is amongst both ADHD, and dyslexic, individuals and to recognise that it is not due to laziness or stupidity. Forgetfulness and distractibility are the manifestation of an executive functioning failure in a brain which struggles to remain focused on one task and constantly responds to, and is distracted by, the changing visual and auditory stimuli around them. The ADHD brain can easily become overwhelmed when there are multiple tasks to manage, or when one task becomes significantly larger than initially anticipated. This is a classic failure of mine. For example, on a day-to-day basis I easily manage most of the cooking and catering in our household, but when friends visit and more complex meal preparations are required, I am known to lose the plot. I can even struggle to make intelligent conversation while brewing a cup of tea! Understanding this I will usually plan well ahead of time or arrange to share the load by having guests bring a dish.

In my experience inattentiveness and hyperactivity can be fatal friends. When well directed, a hyperactive brain can get a lot done, while inattentiveness and distractibility can result in many incomplete tasks. The more mundane an activity, the more easily my brain goes off track. Much of the time my brain runs like an unedited moving picture show, sliding randomly from one story to another without completing any of them. In conversations, this trait can leave others lost and confused, so I don't blame them when they tune out. I have good days and not so good days, but to ensure I achieve my daily goals and complete important tasks I can usually rely on my diary; this is the daily task manager that enables me to function effectively. Additionally, I find it helpful to remove any potentially distracting clutter before I begin my project, this visually and mentally increases my ability to focus on the task. As I discovered during my early university studies, listening to music improves concentration by blocking out or minimising potential auditory distractions. These things work for me but might not work for another; each person must seek and discover the most effective techniques for managing their own quirky brain.

In the classroom, while the ADHD child is trying their hardest to pay attention to the key matters of the moment, the behaviour observed by their teacher may suggest otherwise. Whilst experts agree that not all ADHD is the same, there are some commonalities which an experienced teacher can learn to recognise and understand.

ADHD is neurobiological in origin and manifests through physical, mental and emotional responses and behaviours. It impairs our executive functions and causes difficulties with self-regulation of emotions. ADHD children may have extreme meltdowns when stressed, overwhelmed or emotionally exhausted, such as after a stressful day at school when their coping mechanisms have been depleted. In that state, a meltdown can be triggered by any activity or interaction that demands their full concentration. Do not underestimate how much emotional energy it takes them to simply survive one day at school, never mind a whole week. In an environment expecting round-hole behaviour, even one day for this square-peg can be exhausting.

ADHD adults also suffer this, though hopefully have learned to manage their emotional stress better. When I had to commute and work five full days each week, despite loving my job, I would be washed up at the end of the week. I commonly felt quite unable to apply my brain to anything mentally challenging on Saturday; my Saturday brain was 'out to lunch'! Saturdays became critical "me-time", I would become noticeably distressed if someone or something got in the way of this critical recovery time. Mentally relaxing pursuits such as a bushwalk, a bicycle ride, or a swim in the ocean, perhaps followed by a quiet coffee at the waterfront was the perfect medicine.

Parents and teachers, please know that your ADHD child will likely benefit from the opportunity to apply their pent-up energies to a favourite sport. This type of therapy works for dyslexic children too; the amount of effort they must apply to their schoolwork leaves them similarly depleted mentally and emotionally. My dyslexic brother found joy in racing his Hobie Cat; no doubt the razor-sharp concentration required to keep it upright in a stiff breeze was a welcome contrast to a day of reading, writing and arithmetic. For my ADHD brother, trail-riding was the perfect outlet in his teenage years; later it was martial arts he chose to focus on, and which helped him develop an inner calm and remain centred. As his skills grew so did his confidence; ultimately martial arts became his life's work when he chose to share these skills with others.

Apparently, there is Science behind the ADHD condition. It is thought that one of the causes of poor concentration in ADHD individuals may be due to a low level of dopamine. Dopamine is a drug manufactured in our brain; it fuels our positive feelings and ignites our motivation to get things done. Dopamine affects many of our daily functions, including our thoughts and behaviour, memory, learning, sleep, mood, and physical movements.

When we participate in activities that we enjoy, our brain sends out large amounts of dopamine, which stimulates us to do more of this activity. With their low dopamine levels, ADHD individuals are inclined to struggle with focus and concentration when tasks are viewed as either too difficult or complex, or too tedious or repetitive. Essentially, if it doesn't push their buttons, it doesn't get done. When a tedious job must be completed, the anticipation of a reward at the end can be a strong motivator.

Chapter Eighteen

Connecting With Our Quirky Kids

> The magic moment is the moment when a 'yes' or a 'no' can change our whole existence.
> Paulo Coelho

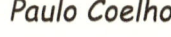

Tragically, due to teachers' misunderstandings, many of our neurodiverse students reach the end of their school journey without ever discovering that there is an identifiable biological cause for their learning difficulties. I am but one example of that.

I become a little excited when I meet or hear of a teacher actively seeking to understand how they can help their neurodiverse students, something their professional training has evidently failed to prepare them for.

Half a lifetime ago, I was one of them, a well-meaning but new and inexperienced teacher, doing what I thought was my best for my students, but deep down knowing it was not good enough for *all*. My professional training did not include any effective instruction that prepared me for teaching the neurodiverse. Unfortunately, this remains true for many graduates today.

For parents of a neurodiverse child, entry to school is frequently the springboard for an emotionally exhausting roller-coaster ride that can last for as long as their child is at school. They suffer heartache after heartache as they witness their previously enthusiastic, happy, and apparently capable child struggling, losing confidence, and becoming openly reluctant to go to school.

Teachers, and parents, may not understand why a particular child is having difficulties; they may assume the child is not paying attention and just needs to work harder. In the best-case scenario, a teacher will recognise something is not as it should be and encourage parents to seek professional advice. Whilst the cost of a professional assessment can be a hurdle for parents and is the reason some are not diagnosed, a lack of diagnosis should not be a barrier to developing a learning plan to support a child who is falling significantly behind. The sooner Accommodations and Adjustments are implemented in the classroom, the sooner that child's anxiety and stress is eased, and they can begin to experience success. Don't misunderstand me, this *is* happening now for some, it is just not the norm.

Whether parenting or teaching them, working with ADHD brained children can stretch the patience and resilience of even the most experienced. For teachers who are encountering ADHD for the first time, it can be stressful, confusing, and even disturbing.

The following considerations are essentially mine but augmented by my many readings and observations over recent years. I share them with you believing that, with greater understanding, the stress for you and your ADHD child or student can be reduced significantly, especially at those times when things begin to turn to lumpy custard. For the most part this involves a change of perspective.

As with Dyslexia, ADHD can be assessed on a spectrum and categorised on a scale from mild to severe. The ADHD brain views their world through their own unique lens; their behaviours and motives are frequently misunderstood. As Gabor Maté says (Maté, 1999), there are two fundamental things that every child, indeed every human, needs and seeks:

attachment and attunement. Both usually come with the love and approval of a special number one someone, typically the mother. When that attachment is healthy, the child's resilience against difficulties is more robust.

With an ADHD child, it is crucial to understand that discipline will not improve any challenging situation but will more likely worsen it; harsh reprimands are likely to be misunderstood. This is true both at home and at school. Time-out is never an empowering or restorative experience for them and being removed or excluded will feel like rejection to that child. A disproportionate number of ADHD children tend to be highly sensitive (Maté, 1999); rather than a motivation to change their behaviour, these children are likely to misread disciplinary measures, which can fuel deeper negative feelings about themselves and their worthiness. Recognise that what these students need from you most is your understanding and support. Their ADHD is not 'who' they are. When they know you believe in them, they begin to believe in themselves, and their self-esteem is reclaimed.

Teachers, please understand that your ADHD student is not purposely being rude when they stare out the window instead of listening to your instructions, or doodle all over the back cover of their mathematics workbook during a quiz. Know that it is not their intention to seem uncooperative, lazy, naughty, or impulsive. Such behaviours are an involuntary manifestation of their ADHD brain in response to a particular situation or environment that they find challenging.

If the sounds and movement around the classroom are particularly challenging for your ADHD student, try to find them a quieter space to work, perhaps at the front of the class, near your desk, if possible, where they can feel more comfortable asking questions. An ADHD child may find noise-cancelling headphones helpful to their concentration.

Sadly, today's teachers are increasingly time-constrained with large classes and additional administrative responsibilities, and I believe that the quality of student-teacher relationships can suffer from this. For our neurodivergent kids especially, a positive connection with a sensitive and understanding teacher is crucial in an environment where they often feel like misfits. Teachers, please take some time to get to know your ADHD student, truly listen to them; acknowledge the positives, appreciate their unique strengths, skills, and talents, and avoid judging them by their behaviours. When they realise you are seeking to understand them, and offering help rather than punishment, their behaviour will change. Okay, it may not be a quick change as building a mutually trusting relationship does take time and effort, especially with children who have come to expect more negatives than positives from their social interactions.

I recommend approaching each apparently challenging situation with questions, rather than assumptions. There will always be a reason, a trigger, an explanation for physical reactions which the child may or may not be able to verbalise at that moment. What could be contributing to their current behaviour? Did they misinterpret the social cues, are they feeling overwhelmed by the task, do they need help to get started on it? Are they frustrated by a buildup of physical energy and need a movement break? Is the noise level around them negatively challenging their attentiveness?

As you learn more about your ADHD child, or student, and build their trust you can help and encourage them develop their own strategies for managing their challenges. Whether a teacher or parent, your fundamental goal is supporting them on their journey towards self-advocacy. Help them develop and follow routines, and encourage them to self-advocate, not only to you, but also to their other teachers. Apply appropriate 'adjustments' to tasks and offer flexible timeframes to enable them to complete each project and experience the satisfaction of success. Permit and encourage them to indicate when they are overwhelmed and need a brain break. Consider whether you can reduce their stress by breaking the activity into smaller chunks.

Most of these principles can be usefully applied to accommodate learning difficulties experienced by any neurodiverse student. In truth, I consider them a part of good teaching practice which will potentially benefit every student in your class, but most particularly those with brain differences such as ADHD, or Dyslexia.

Participating in sport can be a game changer, pardon the pun, for both ADHD and Dyslexia, especially when it becomes part of a regular routine. As well as burning off any inner frustrations created by their school difficulties, it nurtures new skills for which they suffer no disadvantage and have an equal chance of success. As a young teenager, my brother received his dopamine fix from off-road motorcycling; it was a perfect way to burn off his pent-up energy after school. Most weekends he would be off competing against other thrill-seekers, racing over and through rough and untamed terrain. Later he transferred his attention to martial arts which taught him how to rein in his wild mind and train it to focus. For me, badminton was once *the* favoured outlet. Keeping my eyes on that shuttlecock during a fast-moving game left no room in my brain for any other random thoughts! More recently ballroom dancing has provided the perfect outlet for my busy brain and more than satisfied my body's need to keep moving.

Psychologists may give our child's condition a name, but that does not mean we can expect them to behave the same as others with the same diagnosis. Furthermore, many times there is more than one diagnosis in play; as previously noted, ADHD and Dyslexia coexist in approximately 40% of those with Dyslexia. Nevertheless, these remain two distinctly separate disorders and must be diagnosed as such. There will be some overlapping challenges. For example, both Dyslexia and ADHD may cause a child to struggle with a reduced working memory, which leads to difficulty when manipulating multiple bits of information and applying it to a task. For the dyslexic this is due to their reading and writing struggles, and for those with ADHD it is due to their inattentiveness and distractibility, combined with their inability to put the brakes on their racing brain as it flits uncontrollably from one thought or idea to another. They each may suffer anxiety, and overwhelm, and both can easily lose track of time. For the dyslexic, their anxiety may be fuelled by their fear of being judged for their poor reading and writing skills; for an ADHD child, a fear of failure is a constant concern.

I have previously mentioned this, but I cannot emphasise enough how important a professional diagnosis can be for a child. The earlier the Dyslexia, or ADHD, is identified and remediated the better the outcome, mentally, emotionally, and academically. Without intervention there is a real danger that a struggling child may ultimately lose the motivation to try. Understandably, this can have long term consequences as children's self-esteem diminishes, possibly leading to chronic anxiety and social withdrawal. A professional diagnosis builds understanding for the child, and for those who live or work with him; knowing it is not intentional naughtiness or laziness driving their behaviours leads to greater tolerance of their difficulties. Academic failure can have serious life altering effects, training and employment options are limited, and mental health may be compromised. I have yet to work with a dyslexic who is not keenly aware of their underperformance compared to their peers and consequently suffers some degree of reduced self-esteem. Clinical depression is a potential reality for any child with ADHD or Dyslexia; early diagnosis can avoid this. If writing and reading is not developing as expected, or a child is clearly struggling to cope at school, do not hesitate to seek professional advice. Meanwhile, provision of some high-quality remedial intervention will do no harm.

Dyslexia literally means *difficulty with words*. Brain scans have identified a perceptible *physiological difference* between the dyslexic and non-dyslexic brain that can explain these difficulties. (Hudson et al, 2011). Whilst no two human brains are identical, so also there are variations between dyslexic brains. For some dyslexics their greatest challenge is spelling, for others reading, and for many it is both. Some may also struggle with writing, particularly organising their ideas to produce a coherent written script (Dysgraphia), and some also have trouble with mathematics (Dyscalculia). Thinking about the dyslexic brain reminds me of the iceberg analogy. On the outside, one may see a child who is not putting in enough effort, but underneath, they are working harder than anyone else in the room. Because of the physiological differences the dyslexic brain does require a more intense level of explicit teaching to develop their reading, writing and spelling competency and this can be exhausting. This is because they need to build and strengthen *new neural connections* within their brain to enable them to view and recall the symbols accurately and to apply that visual knowledge consistently to their reading and writing. We need teachers to understand how much harder their dyslexic students will need to work at their literacy activities when compared to the non-dyslexic, and how much more practise and repetitions they will need to consolidate and maintain these skills. However, it is important to know that, given the opportunity, most dyslexic individuals can, at minimum, become competent enough readers and writers to complete their education and follow their chosen career path.

Is the dyslexic brain truly different from other brains? Modern medical imaging techniques have enabled close examination of this and, Dehaene (2009), Wolf (2007), and Stein (2006) agree. As Stein explained, when they investigated the reading area of the brain of individuals with Dyslexia, a significant physical difference was observable within the brain's magnocellular area. The difficulty reading words, Stein believes, can be directly attributed to this.

Even from their outward behaviours, the dyslexic brain does appear to have a different way of viewing and interpreting the world. A teacher who can connect with these students and facilitate alternative approaches in their classroom may inspire these individuals to greater learning. Learning is a holistic process; the fluid neural connections between visual, spatial, auditory and kinaesthetic work in harmony and support one another. I have observed that many people with Dyslexia appear to be exceptional visual thinkers; it has been suggested they may be able to view things in multi-dimensional pictures. My dyslexic brother once demonstrated this very ability when he figured out how to fit his new boat, purchased from overseas, into the shipping container, something the exporters had been unable to do. These talents are especially helpful skills for those who take up a career requiring visual acuity, such as design technology; not surprisingly, an extraordinary number of dyslexics do become great artists, architects or engineers.

A cautionary note regarding visual thinking. Whilst many dyslexic brains demonstrate exceptional visual skills, I am not referring to it as a learning style, as with the now disfavoured learning styles theory which categorised students as being primarily Visual, Auditory, or Kinaesthetic (VAK) learners.

Dyslexic children may become competent, even excellent readers and writers, but they must be explicitly taught. They must learn how our writing system works, and that the printed symbols, or graphemes, represent the sounds of speech, in much the same way that the notations on a sheet of music represent specific keys, or notes, on the piano. This approach follows The Science of Reading and is the principle behind the most effective teaching methodologies being advanced today.

Teaching a dyslexic brain to make sense of the squiggles on the paper (the alphabet code) that are used in reading, and learning how to accurately reproduce them for writing, does require a flexible approach to teaching, an adjustment of thinking, and an acceptance that there is no prescribed amount of practise or timeframes for a child with Dyslexia to achieve the skills they need to read and write proficiently. These children will know when they know and not in anyone else's time. If we can exploit their strong visual talents whilst engaging them in activities that use the other senses (speaking, listening, drawing, writing) we help to build and consolidate the neural connections that enable reading skills to progress. Repeated practice will strengthen these neural pathways leading to greater accuracy and fluency, with the goal being 'automaticity'.

Homework can be like poison to a child with Dyslexia. It is not extraordinary for the dyslexic student to be mentally and emotionally exhausted at the end of their school day; after a day struggling to fit in an environment where their differences prevent them from doing so, they need time to unwind and re-energise. I don't recall homework being an issue for me until secondary school when it hit me like a tidal wave. I continually strived to try harder, to apply greater effort, but it never became easier. At the end of each day, my brain was overcooked, and my emotional pot was drained.

Asking these students to complete homework when their day has taken all they have to give can be overwhelming and is unlikely to be productive. For junior scholars (K to 6) the only legitimate homework should be brief and explicitly focused on strengthening their foundational skills, reading, writing and math. Schools generally do not provide individualised teaching for dyslexic students, so they must attend private tutelage either before or after school. For those who come after school our session can be a tough assignment, and it is not unusual for them to demonstrate extreme emotional fatigue; sometimes they are simply too mentally and emotionally depleted to attend. Each time I witness the effects of homework pressure on these hard-working young people my heart aches for them.

I want you to understand that the manifestation of both Dyslexia and ADHD will differ, even between children with similar diagnoses, but please know that all can achieve their potential with the support of an understanding and patient teacher. The classroom will always be a challenging environment, but it is entirely possible to make it less so. When appropriate **Accommodations** are provided for a neurodiverse student, that student is enabled to participate more equitably in the daily classroom learning activities. These accommodations may include resources such as providing a reader-writer, a scan pen, use of a laptop, or changes to scheduling such as extra time for preparation of written tasks and assessments, and time-out breaks in lengthy assessments, such as the Australian National Assessment of Literacy and Numeracy (NAPLAN), which all Australian children must complete in years three, five, seven, and nine. **Adjustments** are modifications made to learning and assessment activities to better enable a student with learning difficulties to demonstrate their skills and knowledge. The intention here is not to 'dumb down' the intellectual requirements but to create a more equitable programme for the neurodiverse student. Providing E-Books or Audio books for class texts, facilitating access to laptops along with writing enablers such as 'voice-to-text', and allowing students to demonstrate their knowledge visually, such as posters and slide shows, will reduce the stresses reading and writing activities create and make success more attainable.

Getting started is normally the most challenging part of any writing task. Writing frames can help with this by giving students a template in which to record their ideas and guide their thinking as they plan their writing, while model texts demonstrate the expected outputs. Many *Accommodations* provided to assist a dyslexic student can also help other neurodiverse students, including the ADHD, whose greatest challenge may simply be to stay focused.

I beg teachers to reduce or remove the need for copying notes from the whiteboard. Dominant memories from my school days, especially in science and geography classes, are of endless note copying. Not only was that task tedious, exhausting and uninspiring but it failed to enhance my learning one bit!

For the dyslexic, especially, working with written text is challenging enough, but having to copy from one text to another creates a whole new level of difficulty. Instead, teachers can reduce their load by providing crucial information on handouts; the most helpful handouts are well-spaced and uncluttered, with a readable font size, 12 or 14. Additionally, allow students extra thinking and planning time for assignments, perhaps with an assignment brief they can take home and discuss with family. Instructional reading material should be decodable and aligned with their skill level, and please don't ask them to read aloud to the class or group, unless they volunteer.

For our dyslexic primary students, aside from the need-based reading and spelling set by their literacy specialist, formal homework is not generally useful. The same is typically true for those with ADHD. These children have worked harder than most just to get through their school day; their mental, and emotional, energy tank is usually drained by the end of the school day and the last thing they need is more torture. More so than many, these challenged children need their breaks, time to have fun playing with their friends and time to be children. I recently learned that one of my young students, diagnosed with Dyslexia and Dysgraphia and who also exhibits ADHD behaviours, has had to forfeit his morning and or lunch break when he does not complete his assigned homework. This teacher is essentially punishing that child for their learning difficulty (disability). I imagine that this teacher believed he was addressing the issue appropriately, but such an approach does nothing to address their learning difficulties and fuels only negative attitudes toward school and teachers, as well as the reading and writing skills they wish to develop.

Some with Dyslexia also have difficulty with the physical process of handwriting, known as Dysgraphia. I wish schools would take the skill of handwriting more seriously. Many schools are now offering digital alternatives for writing, but this is not always an appropriate solution to the difficulties. Whilst keyboarding may address the issues of handwriting legibility, it is not an easy medium to create with. First this option requires that a student is a proficient 'keyboarder', otherwise most of his mental energies needed for organising his ideas will be applied to the keyboard process itself. Second, keyboarding is not so physically connected to the brain's processing centre as handwriting is – ideas flow more easily from the brain through the nervous system directly via the hand on the pencil. Keyboarding creates a neurological 'disconnect'. For the younger dyslexic brains that are still grappling with their spelling and written language skills this can be a problem that only increases their disadvantage.

At secondary level, for teacher-led lessons, electronic versions of course outlines, notes and assignment briefs can be provided in advance of the class sessions to allow extra thinking and preparation time. In particular, the dyslexic brain benefits from extra time to preview and consider the content; however, this approach will also benefit all students. Being prepared this way, they will more readily engage with the material, feel confident participating in relevant discussions and gain more value from the lesson. This method is not new and is known as 'the flipped classroom'. Podcasts of sessions are especially helpful resources; they offer students an opportunity to review and absorb the presentation or discussion at their own pace and time, an invaluable facility for all, but especially for our dyslexic and ADHD students. Oral assessments should be offered at all levels to enable dyslexic students to demonstrate their knowledge more fairly. A combination of both oral and written assessments should be available to ensure fairness where a student's writing difficulties are likely to underrepresent their true level of knowledge. Equity is always our objective. If oral assessment is not possible, a reader writer and extra time allocations will be important support mechanisms.

Almost all dyslexics can learn to write and read. Some have even become writers! Australian author, Jackie French,[5] describes herself as "an historian, ecologist, dyslexic and passionate worker for literacy". She is actively involved in supporting children with learning difficulties and their right to be able to read.

It can be a significant boost to their confidence for a dyslexic child to learn that others who share their challenges with words have overcome their difficulties and become successful. As it is a highly heritable condition, it is very possible they will have a living example within their own family.

---

[5] Home | jackie-french (jackiefrench.com)

Chapter Nineteen

Anxiety and the Neurodiverse

> *Anxiety was born in the very same moment as mankind. And since we will never be able to master it, we will have to learn to live with it—just as we have learned to live with storms.*
> Paulo Coelho

As I cast my eyes over what was to be my closing chapter, I thought I had finished this book but, a few days later, a telephone call from the mother of a past student left me deeply concerned. This addition to my text is my attempt to address the issues she raised.

Over the many years that I have been involved in education, in a professional capacity, the number of identifiable learning and developmental conditions seems to have multiplied so fast that I can barely keep up. Some old familiar syndromes such as attention deficit disorder (ADD) and Dyslexia (SLD) have been renamed and redefined but essentially remain the same. Meanwhile new disorders appear to have been uncovered.

When I was a young teacher, challenging behaviours such as being argumentative and defiant were considered a normal developmental stage of childhood, which later also featured in the teenage years. Now defiance has been labelled Oppositional Defiance Disorder (ODD) and is diagnosed and treated as a systemic behavioural disorder. Disobedience has similarly been re-defined as Pathological Demand Avoidance (PDA) which, rather than a developmental stage, is also a specific diagnosable condition. Defiant behaviours in children pose a significant challenge to parents and teachers. Whilst in the neurotypical, they generally signify the natural emergence of self-will and self-determination, rather than a pathological disorder. They may also appear as serious comorbidities within the diagnoses of other conditions, such as ADHD and ASD. It is my feeling that these behaviours have become chronic in some individuals as a response to feeling out of place amongst their peers, teachers and others, and feeling misunderstood in a world that caters best for the neurotypical.

Anxiety too has become a diagnosable disorder. Most of us experience anxiety at some times in our lives, but for a few it may become a chronic and enduring condition, developed because of significant trauma, which negatively impacts that individual's daily life. For those suffering this way, their anxiety can be mentally and emotionally crippling. For most of us though, anxiety is usually a temporary affliction in response to a single distressing or perturbing situation and the anxiety subsides once the situation has passed. Whether chronic or acute, anxiety can be seriously disabling. For example, during my school days anxiety was the intense apprehension I experienced before and during every school test and examination. I am sure this was triggered by my well-established fear of failing but the anxiety itself became the problem as it created a state of panic in my brain which then interfered with my mental functions and wasted a lot of productive time. Once the exam was over my anxiety was replaced by relief. Is it abnormal to experience anxiety in such situations? I think not.

Managing anxiety at school is a very real challenge for many of our neurodiverse as they must confront their learning challenges daily. For the dyslexic their anxiety, whilst not considered a chronic condition, may be awakened from time to time. These bursts of anxiety are fuelled by their fears. They fear being judged for their poor reading and writing skills or struggling to recall the right words in class discussion, and they fear the potential embarrassment of demonstrating their limitations in front of their classmates. The teacher who asks a dyslexic student to read or present orally to the whole class does not understand the level of anxiety that may cause. For an ADHD child struggling with inattention and impulsiveness, a tendency to become overwhelmed and a working memory that is frequently hijacked by their racing brain, a fear of failure is a constant concern. For that student, avoidance is commonly their favoured strategy; if they don't engage, they cannot fail.

Whilst difficulties with reading is the principal challenge for the dyslexic student, it is not uncommon for that student to also suffer acute stress and anxiety, especially when faced with a situation where their reading or writing is being judged or assessed in front of others. A recent conversation with a concerned parent alerted me to such a situation. Her dyslexic daughter (we'll call her Sam) was preparing for an assessment her teacher required to be delivered as an oral presentation to the whole class. This was a tough assignment, but one Sam was more than willing to deliver. She had put a lot of work into it and was well-prepared, but there was one major concern for her. There were, as in many classes, a small number of students in front of whom she felt very unsafe, the kind who were quick to taunt and make fun of other's mistakes. Sam made one polite request to her teacher, "Please can I present my assignment to a small group rather than the whole class?" Disturbingly for her the teacher refused and pointed out that as 'anxiety' was not included in her Personalised Education Plan (PEP), there was no obligation to make such an adjustment. This caused Sam indescribable distress, which was only resolved after a formal meeting, insisted upon by her concerned and irate parents.

A significant contribution to the dyslexic disadvantage is the lack of deep understanding amongst our educators and a largely inflexible system. Anxiety does not need to be a chronic mental condition for it to have significant consequences for our neurodiverse and our teachers need to be mindful of this when they plan their lessons and assessments. It must be appreciated that all reading and writing activities are at least twice as effortful for a child with Dyslexia than for a non-dyslexic, and any activity with the potential to expose their weakness will be intensely uncomfortable for them.

Additionally, their acute anxiety can in some circumstances overwhelm them so much that the quality of their work is compromised, which increases the degree of disadvantage. Assessment briefs should be clear regarding the specific skills and knowledge they must demonstrate; if it is knowledge being tested then an oral assessment may be the fairest option, but how this is managed should be flexible.

One of my students (currently year 7) was devastated recently when he achieved a score of 27% in a science test. With a diagnosis of Dyslexia and Dysgraphia writing is challenging, but verbally, this student reveals a level of knowledge and understanding beyond the average for his age. Had he been assessed orally I would not be surprised if he had achieved 100%. For this assessment, he had to demonstrate his knowledge only in writing, which immediately placed him at an enormous disadvantage and created unnecessary anxiety and distress.

Every child has a right to a fair and equitable education, and this means accommodating diversity. There is an obligation to provide training for all our educators, and a need for transparency of understanding regarding the concerns and requirements of any student with an SLD. Anxiety must be recognised as a very real and debilitating problem experienced by many. Accommodating student preferences by making 'adjustments' to the assessment tasks is a fair and equitable decision that will avoid unnecessary distress for that student and reduce their anxieties, enabling them to apply all their mental energies effectively to the task. Remember, the first of Maté's principles for teachers is, 'First, do no harm.'

Chapter Twenty

The Mystery Unravelling

> From the moment that you feel enthusiastic about everything, you know that you are following your heart.
> Paulo Coelho

After many years of experience struggling to create order within my quirky and somewhat manic brain, I have accepted that it does not work in the same way as most other brains, and realise that my approach to some things will, from time to time, be misunderstood.

Reflecting on my many years of unfulfilled intentions, I have concluded that the functionality and efficiency of my brain is far too easily disabled by events and situations occurring around me; even when totally engrossed in my task it is almost impossible for me to ignore sounds and movements in my immediate environment. Some of these are beyond my control, such as it was for the nine years I worked in an open-plan office space. I loved my job then but being so easily distracted by noise and movements around me, it was a constant struggle to maintain focus and concentration in that environment. I have long known that I produce my best work when working alone and in a quiet space, but this option is rarely available in the modern workplace, and I have frequently been forced to over-manage my distractibility in a busy environment, usually at the expense of my working efficiency. My chronic distractibility usually means I take longer to complete reports and contracts, so I had to put in more hours, and often took work home.

I wish I had been able to articulate this knowledge and understanding about myself when I was an overwhelmed teenager battling my way through secondary school. In those times, I believed I was incapable of more and came to accept my averageness as the best I could aspire to. Experience has since taught me that my belief was based on false evidence. When my secondary school teachers advocated that I needed to work harder, their views were flawed; what I needed was to understand the true nature of my difficulties and some help to build strategies that could enable me to work 'smarter'. With that knowledge and understanding, my self-esteem could have remained intact and given me the confidence to explore and maximise my strengths.

Academic success only came for me in middle adulthood when fortune offered the opportunity to study and achieve the university degrees I once believed were out of my reach. I have no doubt that I spent longer than most preparing my assignments, but finally realising my academic potential was a turning point for my confidence and self-esteem. It was tempered with a measure of disappointment as I reflected on the lost possibilities of my school days; I began to consider that, had my teachers understood the cause of my difficulties and been able to offer some of the Accommodations and Adjustments currently available, I might have experienced greater success and less angst.

One of my strategies for managing the constraints of my manic brain is to be well organised, I am the *Lady with the List*. Some of my nearest and dearest will describe me as overly pedantic in this regard, but if I don't set parameters for myself nothing gets done. My diary is my best friend and chief assistant who reminds me of my tasks and deadlines, when I remember to look at it! Everything, including laundry and meal preparations, birthdays, special occasions and lesson planning, must be explicitly noted or risk being forgotten. What I have discovered though is that the very act of writing them down seems to create a more delible picture in my mind, so even on those days when I leave my shopping list at home, I can often recall most of my list visually.

Knowledge is empowering; a professional diagnosis can be life-altering. I have lived my life thus far without understanding why my brain worked the way it does (often like an erratic, out of control racing horse), and suffered criticism, self-doubt, depression, shame, and many times a sense of failure, especially when some of those closest to me claim they don't understand me. Many times, I have been called 'scatterbrained'. Unofficially, because I have not been professionally diagnosed, I have concluded that ADHD, with some likely sprinklings of Dyslexia, has likely been my Achilles heel all along. To me, it is the most plausible explanation for the difficulties I had, and still have, with focus and concentration, and the extreme exhaustion I suffered at the end of each school or workday; it serves as a reason for what I had long felt was an ineptitude of my own making. Dyslexia too features in my family genes and may explain my spelling inconsistencies and the inordinate length of time it takes me to produce any significant piece of writing, along with my persistent confusions with left and right.

As I learn more about ADHD and reflect on my childhood, I'm increasingly sure the genetic code for my quirky brain originates with our mother. She exhibited many classic ADHD symptoms, as did my younger brother. Our mother was sensitive, creative, and artistic; she could be cheeky and funny but often preferred her own company. Her greatest loves were her animals and garden. Decision-making was not her strength, and procrastination was her strategy for managing daily activities. I'm sure my mother didn't choose procrastination;

it just happened due to her elastic sense of time. I remember her often saying we would go somewhere "in a minute", but we could wait for as long as an hour, which puzzled me. She was socially reticent, uncomfortable in many social situations, and had only one or two close friends. Mother preferred to be notified of visitors rather than surprises, even from family, and found crowds overwhelming. She struggled to organise herself for special occasions; even the weekly grocery shop was a challenge, and unexpected changes to plans could prove overwhelming.

My younger brother was a clever and quirky child, and his ebullient and unpredictable behaviour was an immeasurable challenge to our mother from the time he could crawl. I do remember his childhood as a whirlwind. He was insatiably curious, constantly active, and could never settle quietly to any activity. Every toy had to be carefully, or not so carefully, dissected to investigate its modus operandi, usually with fatal consequences for the toy! Many times, it drove our mother to a state of desperation; she did not know how to deal with it. I have considered that our mother's difficulty with my brother's somewhat impulsive behaviour was exacerbated by her own mental and emotional challenges of the time. In his younger days, my brother lived constantly on the edge of danger and disaster. At the age of four he had an accident falling from a water tank support structure onto which he had somehow climbed. Apparently, he hit his head in the process and my mother often blamed this incident for his future extreme behaviours. It was our mother's eternal frustration that my young brother did not appear to learn from any of his crazy experiences. Dr Barkley (2016) suggests that the characteristically impulsive ADHD brain is disabled in that it lacks the ability to consider and evaluate potential consequences of their actions; no wonder we don't readily learn from our mistakes!

Whilst it is entirely plausible that ADHD, like Dyslexia, develops from some genetic roots, Gabor Maté (1999) presents us with a fascinating and equally plausible variation to this theory. He proposes that it is not specifically ADHD that is inherited but the sensitivity of character, which is vulnerable to influences of stress and anxiety that may exist while that individual is in their early stages of development. He cites his own childhood experiences, and I find his theory quite enlightening. If your life is touched by ADHD, I cannot recommend his book highly enough.

Our mother was undeniably experiencing some extreme stresses during my, and my brother's, early years – she, with our father, had emigrated from her familiar and much-loved home in England to a strange new country on the opposite reaches of the earth and where they had no family or friends, and had brought only a very few personal possessions. As the youngest in her family our mother had no previous experience with babies, I was her first, and, having been raised in a privileged family who employed a cook to prepare all their meals, our mother had not learned those skills either. One of her early cooking disasters that she was later able to laugh about was when she baked her first batch of scones, using the wooden board as a baking tray! One may imagine the aromas from the oven that day were not as appealing as expected.

Our mother was extremely homesick and struggled to adapt to the changes in those initial years. During my brother's pre-school years, she suffered inconsolable sadness when her father died, and she could not be at home in England at that time. Our mother grew up with animals and loved farm life, which made her well-suited to our rural lifestyle, but I do recall times when she struggled emotionally with the isolation from the homeland she loved so deeply.

When our youngest brother arrived, our parents had purchased a farm of their own; there was a small mortgage, and their budget was tight for a few years. By the time our sister arrived the mortgage had been paid off and our parents were financially secure. They took time out for the holidays, something that had been rare while I was younger, and my sister was able to have the pony she wanted.

During these more settled and secure times, our mother was noticeably calmer and less anxious, although she remained predisposed to procrastination and struggled to organise herself for anything outside the ordinary daily routine. Whilst the older brother and I have worked hard with our stress levels at times, our younger brother is, and has always been, an unflappable character. If we are to accept Maté's theory, the calm disposition of our youngest brother may be attributed directly to our mother's lower levels of anxiety during his younger years.

Whilst the ADHD label brings considerable understanding and validation for me, it has been meeting others struggling with the same kind of quirky brain that has given me the greatest emotional lift. I hadn't made the connection until one afternoon, whilst empathising with one of my students about the challenges of school, she looked at me quizzically and asked, "How come you know this?".

Simply understanding does not instantly improve the executive dysfunctions, but it can improve how one feels about oneself.

Effectively managing ones ADHD requires the application of approaches, such as those I have mentioned in Chapter 15, but, as I well know, these strategies are only as good as one's active attention to them. Some days the wheels still come off, and 'overwhelm' dictates that all my plans are scratched. On such days, the even greater challenge is not to beat myself up for being such a failure!

Life is a journey of constant learning, which is exciting. I have survived the 'school of hard knocks', but still carry some scars acquired along the way. Despite my more than adequate brain I have struggled academically, in employment and socially. As an adult I have, through determined effort, and a few helpful tactics, achieved what my teenage brain did not allow, completing my education and achieving not one but two master level degrees. Additionally, I have now completed a book!

Whilst I am curious, a formal diagnosis requires a psychological assessment and is a very expensive process which I am unable to explore now, but I believe a diagnosis in childhood would have avoided many of the misunderstandings that have been pivotal to my earlier educational and social and relationship failures, not to mention my mental and emotional health along the way.

Chapter Twenty-One

Unravelled and Moving Forward

> There are moments when troubles enter our lives, and we can do nothing to avoid them. But they are there for a reason. Only when we have overcome them will we understand why they were there.
> Paulo Coelho

Several years ago, when restructuring and redundancy left me at a bit of a dead end, I had plenty of time to think and what I thought was that I should revisit my long-held passion for working with dyslexic children. My knowledge about Dyslexia had increased; several members of my immediate family were dyslexic (brother, cousins, nieces), and I lived with a dyslexic! As I began to research the needs and possibilities, it became clear that children with Dyslexia continued to be poorly served in their regular schools. Most teachers had minimal knowledge and understanding, and my recent experiences confirmed that schools remained under-resourced.

So, I began offering 'one-to-one' support to a handful of students who were not doing well at school and had recently been diagnosed with Dyslexia. The response was overwhelming; one day I was hatching an idea, suddenly, I had twelve students, and my days were full. Twelve students may not sound like a large workload but delivering individualised one-to-one tutorials with a dyslexic student is intensive. No two have the exact same starting point, nor the same strengths and weaknesses; planning for one child requires almost the same amount of time as planning for a group or class. Traditional school approaches, such as textbooks and worksheets, are best avoided and replaced by activities tailored specifically to each child's learning needs and dispositions. Many of our activities are intentionally designed to resemble a game more than schoolwork, because fun and laughter reduce anxiety and re-energise the mind; this enables us to practise the explicitly targeted skills in an enjoyable way. Giving my best attention to each child requires a lot of my mental and emotional energy, and I have had to learn to say 'no', which is hard when I am aware of how many unsupported dyslexics are amongst us, with their distressed parents at a loss for a solution.

Advocacy is a significant part of my mission. Whilst teaching their children I am also upskilling the parents, equipping them to advocate for their child as they navigate the many ups and downs of the school experience. The greatest joy for me is watching these young people increase their confidence and begin to realise that, in fact, they are *not* stupid, and they *can* learn to read and write. For their parents, this is so reassuring. I am especially thrilled when their teacher responds positively to the professional recommendations and makes helpful adjustments to classroom activities for that child. However, sadly, this is definitely not the norm

With or without learning difficulties, no two humans are the same in character, desire, intellect, or disposition, not even identical twins, yet our education system continues to offer the greatest rewards to those who can dance the same dance to the same tune in the same way at the same time, the neurotypical way. You might be surprised how few of us fit this category. Those who cannot comfortably blend into this chorus line of the *normal* are fated to spend most of their schooldays battling to belong. Their difficulties may be labelled disabilities, and they are subjected to remedial interventions, which commonly serve only to exacerbate their negative feelings about themselves. Clearly the goal is to 'normalise' them, to upskill them so they can dance that dance. If remedial interventions do not resolve their difficulties, these children must limp along the best they can, believing they will never learn the dance. No wonder that many of our neurodiverse individuals constantly battle low self-esteem, anxiety, and depression.

Some have described Dyslexia as a gift or a 'superpower'. Really? Does anyone honestly believe that their success is due to their Dyslexia? Does anyone with Dyslexia or ADHD truly feel grateful for their almost daily struggle to do what is expected simply to fit in? A dyslexic once suggested to me that it was as much of a gift as being born with one arm. Yes, many dyslexics have discovered their unique strengths and created notable success in their lives, but this has not come from their gift alone but from sheer relentless effort. Each day I work with these unique children I am humbled by their remarkable strength of character and resilience in the face of adversity. Their desire to succeed is supported by willpower and hard work; their different ways of viewing the world and their conscientious determination to meet that reading challenge and complete their education is inspiring. The number of architects, artists, and engineers who live successfully with Dyslexia is a testament to their extraordinary capacity to think beyond the box.

Tiri Language and Literacy evolved from my personal passion. I am passionately opposed to unfairness, the kind of unfairness so many of our dyslexic and ADHD children must face every day at school. My wish is that each of these children learns to love to be who they are and to embrace their uniqueness, acknowledge their own talents and passions, and create a positive future for themselves. This I know they can do, but I also know that they have a better chance of success when they are supported by the unconditional love of their family, and the educated and respectful understanding of teachers who are confident and competent enough to make adjustments to their classroom choreography so all their students may learn to dance in their own way, to their own tune, in their own time, and that is okay.

Working with dyslexic students (many of whom also have ADHD) and their families has deepened my awareness of the enormous challenges faced by more than 15% of our children as they navigate an education system that clearly disadvantages them. Please know that I am not criticising teachers. I have a deep understanding and respect for all classroom teachers; I was one! The tragedy is that most teachers have never been trained to know how to understand and accommodate learning difficulties such as Dyslexia, and few schools are adequately resourced to cater for them.

What I do believe is that every teacher comes to the profession from a position of hope; we hope we have the knowledge, skills, and personality to engage with and help our students on their learning journey, and we hope we can become good, or even great, teachers.

What I learned in my first few years of teaching was that I did not have all the knowledge I needed to help some of my students. What was worse was that I didn't really know specifically what it was that I didn't know, or where to find that knowledge! Too many teachers are in that position today and this must change.

Teaching is a continuously interactive and responsive endeavour. I see the primary role of the teacher as a facilitator of learning; their key goal must be to engage their students in meaningful learning, leading them to form connections between themselves and the knowledge and how it may apply to their lives. Student engagement is critical to the teaching and learning process, and the quality of the student-teacher relationship is critical to engagement. The best teacher will be continuously responsive, always ready to change direction, many times on the spot, to adjust their approach, alter their presentation, or review the context of a teaching and learning activity. Each student brings the opportunity for new learning and teachers need to be flexible; it is unreasonable to expect that one approach will be the best for all. If we desire to be effective teachers, we must continuously evaluate and honestly assess our performance and be prepared to recognise and respond to the different needs that emerge.

Even with my accumulated knowledge to date, I am pleased to say that I am still learning; life would be dull if we ever reached a stage where we no longer wanted to learn or, even worse, thought that we had nothing more to learn. I am sorry to say I have met the odd teacher who sits in that dark closeted space.

You have probably heard reference to learning as a curve, the gentle slope from ignorance to knowledge, from obliviousness to awareness. Sometimes it can come as a sudden jolt, one of those light-bulb moments. Certainly, our most memorable learning curves will be the unexpectedly steep ones, the jumping in the deep end kind of learning experience. However, good teachers will understand that profound and lasting learning is only developed through their involvement over time, motivated by caring, and enhanced and consolidated through practice.

I have taken an extraordinarily long time to wake up to the peculiar mechanics of my own brain, but in the process, I have been privileged to gain tools and knowledge that better enable me to help others learn about their quirky brains and witness their exciting transformation as proudly neurodiverse learners.

On reflection, I can honestly say I would change nothing. I expect there will still be misunderstandings from time to time, but I realise that, without my brain being as it is, without the experiences I have lived, I would not be the same 'me'. Am I suggesting it may be a gift after all? Accepting the quirky me, understanding myself as I do now, certainly has given me access to some unique abilities and opportunities. There is a saying, "*if you love your job then you never have to work a day in your life.*" My only regret is that I did not reach this point sooner in my career.

> "Maybe the journey isn't about becoming anything.
> Maybe it's about unbecoming everything that isn't really you, so that you can be who you were meant to be in the first place."
> Paulo Coelho

A Special Note

I wrote this book out of frustration. My frustration is that our school system does not serve all our children equitably. Children with specific learning difficulties such as Dyslexia and ADHD are especially disadvantaged. These children represent a significant proportion of our school enrolments. With the right teaching and support they can excel, but our schools currently have limited resources, and alternatives are costly for parents.

I believe there are changes that could benefit *all* our students and particularly improve the school experience for those with Dyslexia or ADHD.

- Establish a quality phonics-based system for teaching reading and writing.
- Conduct a phonics check with all Year One students.
- Ensure Accommodations and Adjustments are applied consistently for all students who need them throughout their schooling.
- Provide specific training for all teachers, new and practising, regarding the recognition, understanding of and support for children with these SLDs.
- Provide some financial assistance for dyslexia assessments (for those who need it).
- Allow children with Dyslexia the option to be exempted from second language requirements.
- English language conventions (grammar, spellings, vocabulary, morphology) to be taught at all levels from K-12.

Afterword

This story is entirely my own, shaped by my heart and mind, and seen through the lens of my personal experiences. As is true for all human stories, others who appear along the way may have experienced these moments differently. The opinions expressed are mine alone — some supported by expert voices, and others grounded in my lived experiences.

As I explored in Chapter 21, building meaningful connections with our students is at the heart of effective teaching and learning. For teachers, this is our first and most vital challenge. When we recognise that students with learning differences such as Dyslexia or ADHD often carry emotional injuries like low self-esteem and anxiety, the need for deep, trusting relationships becomes even more critical.

While my journey began with a focus on Dyslexia, as the story unfolded, the significance of ADHD naturally emerged. In Chapter 15, I explored the connection between these two conditions and how they can sometimes complicate a clear diagnosis. In Chapter 17, I shared professional insights into typical symptoms and behaviours, offering a broader understanding.

Sharing these personal experiences has required courage. There were many moments of hesitation, but an inner determination to shed light on the 'misunderstood' — to offer knowledge, compassion, and encouragement — kept me moving forward. Whether you are a teacher, a parent, or perhaps someone who identifies with the 'quirky' among us, I hope you have felt the heart behind this story and found something within these pages that resonates with you.

This book is not intended as an academic reference but rather as a heartfelt letter from me to you — planting seeds of awareness and understanding for those who are so often overlooked. If, as I hope, my story has sparked your curiosity to learn more about Dyslexia, ADHD, and the beautiful complexity of human difference, I encourage you to explore the references provided throughout these pages.

May your learning journey open new windows of understanding — and let the sunlight flood into your soul.

With warm wishes,
Phillipa

About the Author

Phillipa is the oldest of four children, a mother to one daughter, and a grandmother and step-grandmother to six. Phillipa's parents had only recently arrived in New Zealand when she was born (almost two weeks late) in Palmerston North Maternity Hospital. For the first ten and a half years of her life, Phillipa's parents were share farmers in and around the central North Island. Their farm contracts were generally of short duration, often only one or two seasons, which led to frequent changes of homes and schools for Phillipa and her first brother, as well as a disjointed social life. When she was eleven, the family moved eastwards to the other side of the Kaimai Ranges, near Tauranga, where they took ownership of the farm that became their family home for just over forty years.

Phillipa's educational journey has been a bumpy one. At home she was an inquisitive, creative and chatty child who loved books and questioned everything. At school she quickly learned to read but struggled to plan and organise her writing and found mathematics entirely baffling. Her secondary school days were especially challenging and exhausting. Phillipa was near graduating with no idea of a career path until, with the encouragement of an influential teacher, she applied for teachers' training college.

Phillipa is a passionate advocate for those with Dyslexia and ADHD and provides advice and support to students and parents.

With a Diploma in Teaching (Primary), a Graduate Diploma in Tertiary Teaching, a Master's Degree in Education, and another in Adult Literacy & Numeracy, Phillipa's qualifications and experience cover three sectors of education.

Writing this book was an unintended outcome from a presentation paper she wrote for the local minister of education. After hearing many heart-wrenching stories of the struggles dyslexic students faced every day at school, Phillipa wanted to do something to raise awareness and awaken change in schools. During her advocacy work she discovered a large percentage of those with Dyslexia had also been diagnosed with ADHD. Interestingly, the more she worked with these children the more Phillipa began to realise why she identified with them so strongly.

Currently, Phillipa lives with her husband in Western Australia. Their home sits snugly amongst five tranquil acres of beautiful native trees and bush, inhabited by a delightful array of native birds and animals. Regular visitors to their garden include cheeky galahs, cacophonous kookaburras, magnificent black cockatoos, masterful magpies, gentle kangaroos, enchanting brushtail possums, and fascinating bobtail lizards.

Phillipa can be contacted via:
Facebook: Dyslexia at the Tirinui Learning Cafe
email: phillipa0925@gmail.com

References

ADHD Australia. Australian Resources. www.adhdaustralia.org.au/resources/australian-resources/

ADHD Australia. (2021). Building Brighter pathways: ADHD Australia Education Survey Report. Preliminary report. Building-Brighter-Pathways-ADHD-Australia-Education-Survey-Preliminary-Report.pdf (adhdaustralia.org.au)

ADHD Australia. (2020). ADHD Australia National Survey Report: the voice of the ADHD community (2020). Highlighting the Gaps and Priorities of ADHD within Australia. ADHD_Report_12_AF_Digital.pdf (adhdaustralia.org.au)

Axline, V. (1964 & reprinted 1986). Dibs in Search of Self. Ballantine Books. US. ISBN: 9780345339256.

Berlin, R. 1883. Berlin, R. (1883). Über dyslexie. *Medicinisches Correspondenzblatt des Württembergischen Ärztlichen Landesvereins*, 53, 209. Cited in Bennett A. Shaywitz et al. Oxford Review of Education. Published online: 13 Aug. 2020.

Brown, L. (2018). ADHD in Primary School. Perth, WA: Thriving with ADHD. Downloaded from WA: Thriving with ADHD. Downloaded from: https://thrivingwithadhd.com.au?p=3183

Barclay, R. (2016). Managing ADHD in School: the best evidence-based methods for teachers. Pesi Publishing & Media. US.

Paulo Coelho. (n.d.). AZQuotes.com. Retrieved October 02, 2024, from AZQuotes.com Website: https://www.azquotes.com/author/3041-Paulo_Coelho

Dawson, P., Guare, R. (2009). Smart but Scattered; The Revolutionary "Executive Skills" Approach to Helping Kids Reach their Potential. The Guildford Press. New York.

Denny, L. (2023). Literacy and the School-to-Prison Pipeline. Literacy and the School-to-Prison Pipeline (lisadenny.com.au)

Dehaene, S. (2009). Reading in the Brain. The new Science of how we read. Penguin Books Ltd. London and New York.

Eagle, P. (2008). Unravelling the Mysteries of the Great Learning Divide: Barriers to Learning. Massey University Press, Wellington.

Ferrari, J. Dr. (2010). Still Procrastinating: The No Regrets Guide to Getting it Done. Trade Paper Press.

French, J. Home | jackie-french (jackiefrench.com)

Freed, J. and Parsons, L. (1998). Right-Brained Children in a Left-Brained World: Unlocking the Potential of Your ADD Child.

References

Frohlich, C. (2014) Dyslexia: A Time for Talent. The Ultimate Guide for Parents and Children.

Grattan Institute. (2024) Australia needs a reading revolution. Australia needs a reading revolution (grattan.edu.au)

Hudson R.F., High, L. Al Otaiba, S. (2011). Dyslexia, and the brain: What does current research tell us? The Reading Teacher, 60(6), 506-515

Hunter, J. Stobart, A. & Haywood, A. Grattan Institute (2024). The Reading Guarantee: how to give every child the best chance of success. The Reading Guarantee: How to give every child the best chance of success (grattan.edu.au)

Kussmaul, 1877. Kussmaul, A. (1877). Chapter XXVII. In H. von Ziemssen (Ed.), *Cyclopaedia of the practice of medicine: Vol. XIV: Diseases of the nervous system and disturbances of speech* (pp. 770-778). William Wood. Cited in Bennett A. Shaywitz et al. Oxford Review of Education. Published online: 13 Aug. 2020.

Lashlie, C. (2003). Journey to Prison. Who Goes and Why. 2nd Revised Edition. HarperCollins Publishers. ISBN: 9781869504748

Maté, G., 1999. Scattered Minds, The origins, and Healing of Attentions Deficit Disorder.

Office of the Auditor General. Western Australia. (2021). Improving Prisoner Literacy and Numeracy. ISSN: 2200-1913 (print). ISSN: 2200-1921 (online). Improving Prisoner Literacy and Numeracy - Office of the Auditor General

Stein, J. (2006). The Neurobiological Bais of Dyslexia: The Magnocellular Theory. (PDF) The Neurobiological Basis of Dyslexia: The Magnocellular Theory (researchgate.net)

UNESCO. 2024. Key data on girls and women's right to education. Key data on girls and women's right to education | UNESCO

Walker, J. (2002-3). Sounds Write. What is Sounds-Write? - Sounds-Write . Our History - Sounds-Write

Wolf, M. (2007). Proust and the Squid. The Story and Science of the Reading Brain. HarperCollins Publishers.

Acknowledgements

I am enormously grateful to everyone who has helped and guided me towards the completion of this momentous project, my first ever book.

I am particularly appreciative of the creative work from my friend Jennifer Riley. Her inspired painting has become the perfect cover design, and her intricate black and white sketches provide both intriguing visual distractions and some tangible connections to the text.

The sun was shining in my corner when I happened upon Natasa and The Ultimate 48hour Author team. Never did I imagine the publishing process could be so straight forward, and pleasurable too. Thank you Natasa and your publishing 'family', I cannot recommend you highly enough.

A special thank you to the parents who have trusted me to help their children discover their ability to read and write, and to those children with whom I have been privileged to share a little of their journey.

Phillipa Eagle

is a passionate advocate for children with Dyslexia and ADHD. In her recently published book, A Life Misunderstood, she shares her understanding and personal experiences surrounding these learning difficulties.

Phillipa's qualifications and teaching experiences span three sectors, primary, secondary and tertiary, but she is particularly enthusiastic about helping children with dyslexia repair their damaged self-image and realise their potential as readers and learners.

Phillipa left school to train as a primary school teacher but abandoned it four years into her career. Whilst she loved working with the children she felt ill equipped to deal with the large classes as well as the varied and complex mix of learning and behavioural difficulties she encountered.

Phillipa's own school experiences were mixed, she particularly struggled with secondary school. Her achievements were forever impaired by poor concentration, distractibility and inattentiveness - it has taken half a lifetime to recognise that ADHD may have been at the root of all her difficulties.

Phillipa stepped away from teaching to explore other paths but many years later she returned with the determination to help these misunderstood children. During her advocacy work Phillipa has heard many heart wrenching stories about the daily struggles faced by dyslexic children, and their parents, as they navigate the bumpy road to and through school. Additionally, she discovered that a significant number of those with dyslexia were also diagnosed with ADHD, a condition completely misunderstood by most.

Did you know that as many as 20% of children will be affected by either or both these brain-based differences and most teachers feel inadequately trained or resourced to effectively help these children.

Phillipa's book was motivated by her desire to help raise understanding amongst teachers, school leaders, and political decision-makers. She petitions the need and the possibilities for changes within schools to improve the school experience for those with dyslexia and ADHD.

Phillipa is keen to speak to interested groups, large or small, to share her accumulated knowledge and understandings about these common learning differences.

For **teachers**:

- Are you battling to meet the needs of some of your struggling students? Perhaps you have heard of ADHD and dyslexia but want to know and understand more about them. Are you searching for practical strategies and ideas to help these students find their strengths and reach their potential?

For **parents** and **carers**:

- Are you a parent or carer of a child who is having significant difficulties with reading and writing? Perhaps you don't understand the reasons for this, you are possibly confused by the apparent mismatch between your child's verbal competence and their difficulties at school. Maybe you are tired of the fight to have their learning needs met at school but unsure where to go for help.

Phillipa connects with her audience through humour and passion, presenting her stories with a raw honesty that will touch the heart of every caring teacher or parent.

Dyslexia at the Tirinui Learning Café
phillipa0925@gmail.com.au
0436407060

www.ingramcontent.com/pod-product-compliance
Lightning Source LLC
Chambersburg PA
CBHW020407080526
44584CB00014B/1220